BAG OF

Mixed Stories of Life as a San Francisco Punk
in the early 80's

Book two of a punk trilogy

by Ruby Dee Philippa

EARTH ISLAND BOOKS

Published by Earth Island Books

Pickforde Lodge

Pickforde Lane

Ticehurst

East Sussex

TN5 7BN

www.earthislandbooks.com

First published by Earth Island Books 2025

The Vandals 'Urban Struggle/I Want To Be A Cowboy' Credits:
© Written by The Vandals

ISBN 9781916864580 paperback

ISBN 9781916864597 ebook

Printed and bound by Solopress, Southend

Dedication

To Annabelly. You were, and remain to this day, the best of the best.

Author's Note

For those of you who never stepped foot inside the punk rock world of the late 1970's to early 1980's, this collection of short stories might hold some surprises for you. Sure, there were off-the-beaten path experiences and great music and all sorts of crazy shenanigans, but there was a darker side to that way of life too. A lot of the punk rockers I knew were estranged from their families of origin, often lived on the streets, and turned to heavy drinking and drugging along with all the other trappings of being a punk rocker.

For those of you who did live that life, please be aware that some of the stories you read here may be disturbing in their stark descriptions of drug use. I wrote it like I remembered it and didn't pull any punches. So if you think you might be triggered by any of what this collection of stories offers, please partner up with a reading buddy, or make sure you have someone lined up as support you can turn to as needed.

It's my intent to bring this part of my history- and that of many others- to light; not to shock or harm anyone in any way. My cohorts from the time and I have kept in touch over the years, and eventually some of the story-swapping we shared in our reminiscences led to my penning these tales. In our conversations, we all agreed that there is a need for these stories to be told. Hopefully you enjoy reading them as much as I did writing them. Please stay safe in all ways while doing so.

Contents

Acknowledgement

Here's to all of those who shared the streets, squats, dumpsters, punk venues, and other assorted and sundry locales for our adventures together back in the day. You inhabit my memories and provided fuel for the fire that ignited these stories. I could mention names, but honestly, you know who you are. If you recognize yourself in any of these characters, I hope you see that I recall the good parts as well as the not-so-good. And of course, most importantly, I want to thank you for being a part of that crazy dance we called life, and for helping to carry the memories of those we have lost.

BAG OF TRICKS

Mixed Stories of Life as a San Francisco Punk
in the early 80's

Book two of a punk trilogy

by Ruby Dee Philippa

"Maybe I'll go where I can see stars, he said to himself as the car gained velocity and altitude; it headed away from San Francisco, toward the uninhabited desolation to the north. To the place where no living thing would go. Not unless it felt that the end had come."
— Philip K. Dick, Do Androids Dream of Electric Sheep?

We Could Be Heroes

1

Amy rolls over in her dirty sheets; greasy from months without soap and water and greyed with age. She reaches over her head for the letter resting on the long single shelf along the headboard above her. Turning over onto her back, she peers at the letter, front and back, again.

She still hasn't decided what to do. She opens the sharp triangle of the envelope flap, pulls the letter out, and places the envelope on her stomach as she prepares to read the note again.

Dear Lil' Sis,

I hope this letter reaches you. We've been having a hard time getting in touch with you. Mom and pop are worried. I guess you dropped out of college, since pop got a letter saying as much. Just so you know, I don't blame you. But I'm worried too. I hope my lil sis is doing alright.

Mom and pop are flying me out to San Francisco to come visit you. Mostly for them it's for me to come spy on you. Mostly for me it's to see if you're ok or if you need anything. I arrive in San Francisco Monday November 6th on Air Canada 103 at 13:30. If you can't meet me at the airport, let me know where we can meet after.

I really miss my little sister. I hope everything is ok. By the way, if you are ok, I'm going to spank you for making us all worry so much.

See you next week,
Robert

Amy worries a corner of the letter beneath her thumbnail, cleaning a stubborn bit of dirt there. She rolls over and peers out the grimy window across her room that looks onto the back porch and over their tiny sliver of backyard. She doesn't know what time it is, exactly, but she's sure it's morning. The fog has that hazy yet bright morning light refraction that Amy finds comforting and safe. She sighs, and rolling over again, sits up.

Damnit. This is Robert, her favorite older brother. She has

to go meet him, which means she has to get moving now, in order to get her head straight, and get to the airport on time. But still, she pauses. She's afraid of what he's going to think when he sees her. The last time she was home, before he helped her move to San Francisco to attend school a little over a year ago, she easily weighed fifty-six kilos. Now, she's not sure, but she thinks she can't tip the scales at more than forty-three.

She used to be not exactly muscle-bound, but she had muscles from doing her chores around the farm. And now her arms are like pencils. Her legs are doing ok from all the skating she does, but she's too skinny and she knows it.

Amy walks over to the round orange plastic-framed mirror on the wall and studies her reflection. She shrugs. Robert will probably get a kick out of her hair- or lack of it. But she looks bad. There was something in that last batch of speed going around that caused her skin to come off in sheets, like a sunburn. She has blotches of mottled red and white patches around her neck and shoulders, like birthmarks where there were none before. Luckily, it's cold outside, so she can easily cover that up with a high collar, or a scarf.

Ok, let's get this show on the road. She turns around and studies the organized chaos of her room. Magazines are piled up in crazy leaning totems along one wall- a scissors-

and-glue speed project she hasn't had a chance to get to yet. Her clothes are more-or-less where they belong, in various states of folded or semi-folded and draped inside and out of four milk crates from Petrini's Market, stacked two by two next to the door. Her board rests on its tail against the crates. And everything else is scattered across the filthy rug in her own version of where things belong-plastic makeup cases in this corner, scuffed black boots, red and white sneakers, and crumpled socks over there, scraps of photos and string and bits of leather from past speed projects she hasn't quite finished piled near the foot of the bed, and empty Pepsi bottles and greasy McDonalds' paper bags half-heartedly organized in a few piles she keeps intending to deal with later on.

Amy picks through her clothes and chooses a soft black English army shirt that reaches almost to her knees, a pair of mostly clean black long-john leggings, and the least crunchy socks she can find. She drops the t-shirt she wears to bed atop her greasy, flat pillow, and turning her back to the window, gets dressed. At the mirror, she turns up her collar and attaches one corner over the other across her throat with a safety pin. There, that will cover her blotchy skin. It doesn't itch any more, but man, while the drugs were making their way through her body, she'd felt like she was on fire, and couldn't stop grabbing little edges of skin that were peeling away from her neck. Pulling, pulling,

pulling until they came off in sheets, translucent and marked with tiny faint rivulets, like butterfly wings. She'd been so embarrassed, she hadn't even said anything to Val and Sophie, worried they would make a fuss over her. She wore scarves or bandanas around her neck for a week.

Amy clears a spot on the floor and sits down to pull on her socks. She wrinkles her nose. They smell pretty bad but they'll have to do. She leans over and deciding on her Doc Martens, pulls open the laces and wriggles her feet into place. One boot at a time, she pulls the laces taut, loops the extra lengths around her calves, and ties each with a neat little surgeon's bow, exactly the way Robert taught her.

Grabbing her small, brightly colored Gujarat bag hanging from the big S-hook on the back of her bedroom door, Amy quickly opens it to check that A) her passport is in it, B) she has some cash for the bus and BART to the airport, and C) there are no drugs. Check, check, and check. She loops the bag over her head and one shoulder, across her chest, then looks around her room once again before she steps out to see what time it is and what her next move should be. Oh right! She grabs the M77 bullet belt hanging over the door handle and wraps that around her hips. Clicking the lipstick link into place, she shifts the belt back on her hips so the bullets don't poke into her legs.

Amy pauses, then softly turns the door handle and pushes down on the knob as she opens it quietly. She's surprised her roommates plenty of times and doesn't like to freak them out by popping in on them as they're at the sink or bent over peering into the nearly-always empty fridge. Ok good, no-one here. Amy's not quite ready to share her family with her friends, not until she susses out how to explain what she's done with herself over the past year. She glances at the plastic cat clock on the wall above the table, with its broken tail that used to swing back and forth. It's not even 10am yet, earlier than she thought.

She has time, so slight change of plan. Amy grabs her board, and makes her way quietly out the back door, across the porch, and down the stairs. Once on the street, she skates distractedly, pensively making her way to Café Cantata on Haight. There, she orders a small coffee with an inch to spare and loads it up with cream and sugar to satisfy her speedster sweet-tooth.

Out front by the bench and planters lined up beneath the broad picture window, Amy parks her board and folds herself up to sit on it, gliding side to side gently as she drinks the coffee and stares out blindly into the street. She can feel her brain shutting down, her emotions tucking themselves neatly away into that box she's created since she started doing so many drugs. Since she stopped calling and writing her family. Since she changed into who she's become. Shit, she's scared to see Robert. She's afraid of what he will think of her and say about it. She's afraid he'll decide he doesn't like his kid sister anymore.

She finishes the cooled coffee, sighs, and stands up to throw the cup away. One foot on the board to ease it off the sidewalk and onto the street, Amy starts to skate, picking up speed until she's moving pretty fast, a bit too fast, towards the Civic Center, downtown. She usually enjoys this ride- mostly downhill and travelling across different parts of the City. But today, she's grinding her teeth and barely notices the street signs as she flies by.

Down Haight to Market, left on Market, zipping past parked cars, buses, and pedestrians who recoil as she barrels past, skating recklessly and hard. She doesn't want to arrive at the airport too early and have to sit around, not allowed to skate across all those tantalizing smooth walkways, so she takes a few detours- up Hyde to Fulton, across the Asian Art Museum park. Up, and back. Up, and back. She works up a light sweat and feels her gut un-clench. She's stopped grinding her teeth too. That's better.

She skates back up Fulton across the brick pedestrian plaza and grabs a seat on one of the empty benches this time of day. Amy fumbles in the pocket of her Gujarat bag for her cigarettes. Last one, shit, she'll have to pick up some more somewhere. She smokes the cig, then hops back on her board and skates lazily over to the BART station across the plaza.

From there, Amy buys her ticket, boards the next train just arriving, and settles in for the thirty minutes or so it takes to get all the way out to the San Francisco airport. With her board held firmly between both knees, Amy chews on the pad of her thumb, and begins to worry again. She wishes she had thought to wear a hat. Maybe Robert won't like her shaved head after all. She wishes now that she had one of the Clits with her. Val would probably be cool and help distract Robert.

At the airport, Amy heads into the International terminal, and locates which gate will be vomiting up a stream of people from flight 103. Carrying her board tucked up tight at her side, she walks determinedly along the loud, clickety-clackety echoing causeway, filled with bright and shiny shops full of bullshit no-one really needs, but she looks anyway. She arrives at the gate with minutes to spare, so she leans against a large, cool column in the middle of the walkway, holding her board lengthways against her leg, and waits.

Minutes pass quickly, and Amy alternates chewing on her lower lip and the pad of her thumb. Lip, thumb, lip, thumb. She notices a little boy in a Dennis the Menace striped t-shirt and dungarees staring straight at her, nothing shy about this little guy. Amy screws her face up into a goofy grin, half-way crosses her eyes and sticks her tongue out. The little boy jumps up in his seat, he knew she was there to amuse him! Amy smiles happily and turns her attention to the gateway that has started to trickle in, then flood with passengers exiting the plane. Not him. Not him. Definitely not him... she looks down at her body- shirt, leggings, socks, boots, floor. Then back up, lower lip captured beneath her top teeth. Come on...

And there he is. Amy's heart jumps in her chest. Oh! There's her big bro! He doesn't see her yet, giving her a chance to look him over before they start their visit or whatever this is. He looks good. He looks great, even. His sandy blond hair is a little longer than it used to be, with a faint curl over his forehead and at his neck. He's wearing new jeans, a thick wool button up shirt in a light tan plaid, and his standard Timberlands. Amy raises her arm in greeting and steps away from the column.

She watches as the expression on his face goes from blankly searching searching searching past where she is standing, to pause, refocus, and a sudden, deep narrowing of his eyes as he fixates on her again. "What the fuh...?" Oh no. "Amy?!!" He walks straight for her, grinning that lopsided grin. And hey, his eyes are sparkling. He's happy to see her!

She steps forward, and holds one arm out to hug him, clasping her board against the length of her leg. She's so glad she wore this shirt. She hopes the rash doesn't show.

Robert wraps his arm around Amy's shoulder and pulls her in for a quick bear hug, catch and release. He pulls her out of the way of people moving around them, up against the column. "Oh my God. Amy, what did you do to your hair?" She ducks her head, grinning slightly. "This is the way all my girls wear it. Not every girl I know. Just... my girls. My friends." She leans away from him, searching his eyes. "Do you like it?"

He leans back slightly and cups the elbow of one arm while stroking his chin in mock-consideration, "Hmmmm... let me see... yes! I like you being a crazy baldie!" Then he touches her shoulder again. "Though Lil' Sis, you need to eat a cheeseburger. Or three."

They follow the signs to the right luggage carousel, locate their mother's avocado green hard-shell suitcase that she lent him for the trip, and find their way to the train back to the City. Since Amy never wrote or called after receiving his letter, Robert had made reservations at a cheap motel over on Lombard. Amy explains how out of the way that is from her place, but she's relieved. He doesn't have to see the squalor where she lives. They study the train routes, and catch up, more-or-less, staying away from the bigger topic of what the hell she's doing and what the hell happened to school, and focus on easier subjects How's the farm. How are mom and dad. How the other brothers and cousins are doing. How the horses and their favorite cow are holding up after a brutally hot and dry summer this past year.

Once they arrive at his motel, they hang out in his room on the second floor, with the oceanic sounds of Lombard streaming by outside. Robert confesses that he is going to leave the farm and attend Algonquin to get his Bachelor's Degree in Public Safety starting in the Spring. So her big brother is going to be a cop. Amy really wants a cigarette now. If it's time to explain what happened with school and her apartment and her life, she'll need a cig.

She checks her bag to make sure she has enough for a pack from the machine downstairs outside the front desk. "I'm getting some cigarettes. Do you want anything?" Robert reaches for the phone. "Nah. I think I'll order a pizza. You want to split a Hawaiian?" The idea of food clenches Amy's belly again, but in lieu of doing any speed, yeah, she supposes she should try to eat something. Especially so Robert doesn't get suspicious.

She grabs her handful of change and run-skips down the stairs, buys her death-sticks- they have Old Golds!-

and clomps back up to Robert's room, hoping there are matches there.

Robert has kicked off his boots and leans against the headboard of his bed with his legs splayed out before him. Amy nervously grabs matches from the ashtray on the bedside table and lights up. Then she starts fidgeting, she's so nervous. She sits on the edge of the bed facing Robert. She lies back. She rolls over onto her stomach and flips her feet up into the air. She chews her thumb and drags on the cigarette. And suddenly, before she can stop herself, she starts spilling- fessing up to her big bro what led her to drop out and fall out of contact with everyone back home. She can't look into his eyes too long, so she looks at the ceiling and at the floral pattern of the bedspread. She's certain he's deeply disappointed. But she can't stop now that she's started, so she talks and talks.

2

She tells him how alien she felt the first few weeks on campus. How she felt like people were staring at her and making fun of her as she walked by. Hick, Rube, Podunk. She had her small routine: wake up, get coffee, go to class, eat something at one of the campus cafeterias or vending machines, go back to the apartment, study, sleep. She was lonely, and a little frightened. Not of anyone or anything in particular. Just uncomfortable and skittish of everything around her.

Then she met Henry, and he introduced her to his friends. She started going to shows and hanging out with people who accepted her for who she was, not for who they thought she was going to become. She shaved her head and bought her board and stopped going to classes. Well, honestly, she'd been having a hard time with two of her classes, so dropping out wasn't that far of a reach. When she'd originally decided to study Poli Sci, she'd envisioned going overseas and helping malnourished children, helping villages learn to farm, and making things better in the world.

But the classes she was taking fed none of that dream. One class focused on International Terrorism, and forced Amy to look at photos and films and read articles about things she'd never wanted to see or know. Another class that she couldn't relate to in any way was a Business class, of all things. She had to take it, as it was part of the required curriculum, but she never understood why. She couldn't follow the concepts and theories and had absolutely nothing in common with any of the bozos who were in the class with her.

At first, she figured she would stop taking just those classes and make up for them by switching her major. She could fulfill the new requirements the following semester. Then things slipped away from her. She started spending more and more time at the Clits' house, which was far enough away from campus to make it hard for her to make it to any classes after a night raging at a show, skating the streets, and doing drugs. So she just stopped. Henry helped her move her few belongings into the room behind the kitchen at the Clits' house, and then... well, then almost a year has gone by, without Amy even realizing it.

She pauses and looks directly into Robert's eyes. Funny, she's shaking, but she doesn't feel nervous anymore. Amy realizes that she wasn't worried about what her mom and dad might think. Only Robert, and now he knows what she's done with herself. And the verdict is... she wonders, as Robert nods his head, pondering on what to say and how to say it.

"Well," he sits up and places his feet on the floor. "You seriously fucked yourself up, Lil Sis of mine." He shakes his head rhythmically, side to side. "Now, how we gonna fix this?" With his eyebrows raised and his head tilted to one side, he observes her. Amy doesn't know what he's asking. Does he want an answer? She chews her bottom lip and waits.

Robert shrugs and lifts both hands palms-up in query. "You want to come back to Ontario with me? We could rent a car or a van- how much stuff do you have? And you could come home with me!"

Amy shakes her head and looks down at the floor. "I don't think that's such a good idea, Robert. I can't go back to the farm. Mom and dad can't see me like this. I can't see them... not like this." She waves her hands at her body and lets out a deep sigh.

Robert leans in. "I'm not saying go back to the farm. You just told me how unhappy you are. Come with me to Ottowa. You can stay with me. I only have a one bedroom, but there's a fold-out couch... or a huge closet that could be a tiny bedroom. Big enough for you, how scrawny you are now..." He shakes his head again. "I mean, you could come stay with me, get better, and then if you want to, go to University there! We could be heroes, and both graduate together!" He's worked himself up and excitedly rubs his hands together. "Please Lil Sis? Come home with me!"

Amy considers his proposition silently. She didn't exactly say she was still unhappy. But she realizes, she is. She'd been happy for a while. When she and Henry had skated tough together, it felt like they'd ruled the streets at night. When she first began to get to know Sophie and Val, she'd felt so much less alone, so included. And when she first started snorting and then shooting speed, that was a different kind of happiness. Happiness forced into her veins, popping out of her pores like one of those clowns that jump out of a box. What are those called? Ah... Jack-in-the-box happiness. Pops out on drugs so you push it back in. But the drugs haven't made her happy for a while now. And Henry has moved on. They see each other at shows and in passing, but that's not the same at all. And of course, Sophie has pulled away, now that she and Henry are together. Even Val, funny, goofy Val, has for some reason un-included Amy from her life, bit by bit.

So no, she isn't happy. "Yeah, ok, I can do that." She sighs again, "I didn't tell you, but there's been some bad stuff going on. Some girl got killed and left in a dumpster. Some crazy lady who thinks she's some kind of witch burned a friend of mine's apartment down. And...uh, this other girl I know was kidnapped and held captive in some weird sex slave deal until she escaped. Yeah... I... I think I'm ready to go home. I'd like that." Amy grins, a wide, soft grin, full of a half-hearted sense of peace that she hasn't felt in a long time. She looks at her brother as tears sparkle at the corners of her eyes, blurring her vision.

The pizza arrives, and they make plans while Amy picks at the pineapple and ham, avoiding the bread and cheese. Robert will rent a van from right up the street and then drive Amy to Pat's house in the Haight. There, she can pack her crates, and there's an old trunk Mouse gave her that's been sitting on the back porch, forgotten. Now she can use it. Whatever doesn't fit in the crates can go into the trunk: her posters, art projects and books. Amy realizes she doesn't own much. She's given up and lost a lot since she tumbled down this path. She and Robert agree it's better to leave her bedding behind.

As Robert finishes his fourth slice of pie, he shoves the last bit of crust into his mouth and reaches over to wrap his hand around Amy's bicep. Forefinger to thumb, he gasps, "Jesus, Amy! I'm serious. You need to quit picking and eat something. What the fuck?"

Amy nods, yeah, she knows. "I'm ok. I promise, I'll be ok. I'm just not hungry right now." She knows she'll need to talk to him about what else she's done to herself. But not right now. Not yet. Maybe he'll forget to ask again? And she can just be ok? "I'll eat, promise. Oh, actually, when we go to the house, can we stop at the market and get some juice? And maybe more cigarettes and stuff for the trip?"

Robert's ok with that, but he's already decided he's going to watch what she does from here on out. He thinks she might be on drugs, though he's not sure what. Diet pills? He's lived his entire life on the farm, and what he knows about drugs he's learned from watching movies and TV. Either way, whatever's going on, he's here now. She's with him, and he's not gonna let his kid sister keep fucking herself up like she's done so far. They'll go home and get her settled in. He'll make her eat burgers every night if that's what it takes.

Robert closes the pizza box and scoots it to the end of the bed. He pulls his boots on, and lacing them tight, says he'll go get a van. Or a car? Does she really only have a few boxes and a trunk? Amy says yeah, that's it. So he heads out, leaving the key. "I'll be right back. If you want, there's a soda machine at the front desk. They might have some kinda juice?" He just wants her to be here when he gets back.

An hour later, they drive the few blocks surrounding Pat's apartment, looking for parking. Around this block, around that block, a few times, until someone pulls out ahead of them and Amy jumps out to stand in the spot so Robert can maneuver the car into place. It's turned into a beautiful evening. The fog lifted some time ago, and time has faded as Amy and her Big Bro share stories and make plans.

Amy brings Robert up the back stairs to the porch. The back door is locked- huh, that's odd. It's never locked, usually. She jiggles the window to her room and it pops up easily. She climbs inside, runs to the back door, and lets Robert in. Her heart sinks- she can physically feel it sinking in her chest as he looks around the garbage strewn, grimy kitchen. At the broken, filthy table, the moldy, food-splattered couch, and the ever-present sink full of greasy, rancid dishes.

Amy pushes the door to her room open, then agh, there's that clenching, sinking feeling in her chest again. She sees her room through her brother's eyes: filthy, uninhabitable. How did she get here?

Robert sees Amy watching him scan her life, and offers, "Hey don't worry about it, kid. Let's get you packed up and let's get outta here. We can pick up supplies for the road, and stay at the hotel, then leave first thing in the morning. Kay?" He touches her shoulder, sharp and balsa-thin. Amy smiles guiltily at him. "I'm sorry. I'm embarrassed by...

this." She slices one hand through the air, including everything on that side of the room.

"No worries. I'm serious." He hugs her lightly, shocked at how skinny she is. Burgers, and omelettes, for sure. He lets go and stands back with his hands in fists at his hips. "Ok, where do we start?" Amy turns and considers, then points at the crates. "There, you can put all that stuff into those crates. Just, everything on them. And, oh... well, they're not clean, but all these socks and my skate sneaks too. Wait, first, can you help me bring in that trunk from outside?"

"I got it. That trunk will crush you. Just get your stuff together."

Amy starts collecting things on her bed, pulling posters carefully off the wall. She stacks books, notebooks, and magazines into careful piles. Her records! She almost forgot her records. She grabs a handful of records from against the wall, then another. There aren't a lot. She traded most of her collection for speed that one time, even though she was already working and had some money coming in. Amy pauses at the makeup cases. Does she want those? Sometimes she wears kohl from this funky little stoppered bottle that she bought up on Haight, or occasionally she'll tweak for hours in the mirror with eye-shadow and liner.

Chewing her lip, she thinks of the day that Shelly gave her that first make-up kit there, full of bright and shiny colors, crazy pinks and blues she would never wear, and tiny tubes of glossy shades of lipstick. Shelly had pointed out the shade she said Amy should wear- this deadly eye-piercing come-fuck-me red. So Amy did, for a while. She painted her eyelids varying hues of gold and copper, dark green and a purple so dark it was nearly black. She would blot circles around her eyes as though she'd been in a bad fight. Yeah, you should see the other guy, she'd grin...

And she wore that come-fuck-me red lipstick. Until the day she saw a lip print in that exact same color on Henry's shirt. And she knew, she knew, that she hadn't kissed Henry there. Somehow, she'd had the courage, instantly, to confront him. And seeing Amy's stance, the determined glint of 'don't fucking lie to me' in her eyes, Henry had quickly come clean. Yeah, that was from Shelly. Yeah, they'd been fucking around some. No, he didn't love her, but hey man... But 'hey man' nothing. Amy had ended it then and there. She threw him out of her room, dropping his things all over the kitchen floor, shaking her hands as though she'd touched something dead.

She'd skated over to Shelly's place then, feeling sick and angrier than she could ever remember feeling before. She'd walked slowly and mindfully into Shelly's apartment, waited patiently for the various customers to get their business over with, and leaned against Shelly's bedroom door as she quietly kicked the door shut behind her. She can't remember exactly what she'd said, only that she'd kept her voice even and low, trying to smooth out the trembling she felt inside. She told Shelly to stay away from her, and to keep her sicko makeup bullshit to herself. She remembers now, she'd also warned Shelly that if she ever heard of her doing that to another punk, she'd come kick her ass.

Ok, that settles that. She'll never touch that makeup kit again. Amy stands in the middle of her room, this room where she's cried a lot of tears, shut out a lot of feelings, done a lot of drugs. She turns around, slowly taking in every surface. Does she need any of this other stuff? She adds a short stack of photos and Robert's letter from the headboard shelf to the few things piled on top of her bed. She turns around again. Nope, nope and nope. There is absolutely nothing of value in this room, except for her brother, standing in the doorway with her trunk balanced on one shoulder.

She moves the piles of books, papers, posters and photos aside and points to the cleared spot. Robert sets the trunk down where indicated and turns his attention to the crates and mess of clothing. Amy drops her few possessions into the trunk, trying to lay them out evenly so nothing gets damaged en route home. HOME! She gets a ticklish feeling at the back of her throat when she thinks of Bytown, and all the trees and rivers and sky. All that green and blue, even if she is in the city. She wasn't a skater last time she was anywhere near Ottowa, so she wonders how that's going to go over. Maybe she can teach Robert how to skate and they can ride the streets together? Get Team Hero patches and cut up some Levis jackets for vests?

She finishes arranging her few things and closes and latches the trunk. She helps Robert finish folding and stuffing the ragged, dirty clothes she'd been so proud of just yesterday into the crates. Maybe after a load of laundry, she'll feel better about them again. Amy takes one more slow gander around the room. Other than her leather jacket with a tear along one arm: That. Is. It. They move the crates and trunk quickly, carefully, down the back stairs and out to the street. Robert runs back upstairs for the other crates while Amy parks herself on the trunk out front. He drops them by her feet and walks off quickly to bring the car around.

Once loaded up, Amy nervously peers up and down the street, worried one of her pals will see them. They pile into the car and head over to Petrinis for juice, cigarettes, chips, and candy- definitely candy, for the trip ahead.

Robert protectively walks by his sister's side. He's not exactly sure what he thinks might happen, but he can hardly wait to get her away from this place and get her home. They push a cart in front of them up and down the aisles, adding potato chips, grape licorice, SweetTarts, Cokes and fresh orange juice. Robert thinks to grab a few apples and oranges too. Amy can't get healthy on any of this other crap. As they turn down the last aisle towards the front of the store, Amy sees Max turn the corner.

He sees her too. "Hey! Wha's going on, stranger?" He lifts his hand in a high five greeting, and Amy complies, slap. She glances at Robert and back at Max. "Max... this is my brother Robert. Robert, this is my friend Max." She nervously chews her lip and tries to smile at the same time. Max holds out his hand, "Good to meetya man. Amy talks about you all the time."

Robert shakes Max's hand and grins, that same sideways grin that Amy has, Max notices. "It's good to meet you too. Sorry we can't stay longer, but..." he looks down at the cart of non-perishables and cracks up. "I mean, we're not staying long." Max doesn't understand. "Where ya going?" Amy holds onto the cart with both hands and rocks up onto the toes of her boots as best she can. "Mmm, Max." He refocuses on Amy's face, something's going on.

"I'm going back to Canada. Robert's helping me move."

Max pauses, what? "What? Since when are you going to Canada? For Christmas? Or... for good?" He thinks he knows the answer. Oh Aims, he begs in his mind. Please, no. Amy nods, "Yeah, it is kinda sudden. Um, Robert came for a visit, and we- I- decided I should head home for a while." She pauses and licks her lower lip. "Well, not a while. I'm going home. Maybe go back to school...? I don't know yet. But Max..." She looks at him, searching for something, a little helplessly.

Robert pushes the cart out of Amy's hands. "Hey, I'm going to go check out. You want Old Golds, right?" He asks and Amy nods yes. She and Max watch him push the cart away and turn back towards one another.

"Well shit. I can't say I'm surprised so much as I'm sorry. Really sorry to see you go." Max leans against the shelf of canned goods, his leather creaking as it adjusts. "Ah, Aims..." He reaches for one of her hands and touches the tips of his blistered fingers to each of hers. Amy suddenly wants to cry, 'why now?!' She presses her lips together in a fake smile, pressing back the tears that are threatening to flow any second. "Well shit, Max," she manages, and with a deep breath, "We can write. You can come visit." She looks around, "I mean, I don't have an address yet, but once I do, I can write to you, and you could come..."

Max laces his fingers through hers, and clasps her hand, palm to palm. With the forefinger of his other hand, he touches the tip of her nose, then brushes her lips, just once, briefly. "Yeah, cool. That sounds alright, I guess. I mean, it's better than nothing." He smiles. "I just, I hoped..." He shakes it off, squeezes her hand and lets go. "I just thought something was gonna happen, you know?" He rolls his shoulders back, making his jacket creak again. "Yeah, write to me. Promise. I'll get the guys to put some shows together up there, or just come and hang out, whatever works out."

Amy grins now. Her tears have retreated safely. She really didn't want to cry, not this last time maybe seeing Max in a long while. "Yeah! I was thinking, I'd teach my brother to skate and I'll make up some colors and vests. You could come up and get an honorary flag!" She looks up into Max's eyes hopefully.

He glances up above her head, and back down into her eyes, "Yeah, that sounds cool. You know, this is kinda shocking. I'm really gonna miss you, Amy." He leans down and kisses her then and there, right in the middle of the canned beans section at Petrini's Market. She leans up and into his kiss, one shoulder brushing against the flap of his jacket. Why does Max taste so good?

They release their kiss, this one kiss. Maybe the only one? Hopefully not. Amy touches her lips and grins off to the side. "Uh, I should probably go. Unless... you want to get some Chinese? I'm sure Robert wouldn't mind. I think he was planning to eat at the motel- he's got a room over on Lombard- and then we're gonna leave early in the morning." She decides, "Yeah, come have dinner with us. Lemme go ask."

Max groans, "Ah no, Aims, I can't. We've gotta rehearse tonight. I wish I could..." She smacks the palm of one hand to her forehead. Right! The Shits rehearse Mondays and Wednesdays at the Tool and Die, downstairs. It's still Monday. "Right, sorry. Ok. I don't want to keep Robert waiting. I promise I'll write to you, ok?" She dances a little in place, eager to get outside and not keep her brother waiting any longer. Max touches her arm and leans in again, one more for the road. They linger a moment, just a touch of lips to lips. Then Max steps back, his hand still on Amy's shoulder.

"Ok Aims. Get out there. Go be safe. And don't make me wait too long, you hear?" He half salutes and walks away, leaving Amy with nothing left to do but look where she's going and walk out of the store.

3

Robert is leaning against the driver's door, arms crossed, eyes closed, humming some little tune to himself. He startles as Amy tries to open the passenger door. "Ah, one second!" She runs over to the donation trailer parked at the side of the store, and paws half-heartedly through a few boxes and bags piled outside the trailer door. Trash, trash, trash... what is wrong with these people? She doesn't find anything, but then again, she's not doing it right. It should be 6 o'clock in the morning, and she should be climbing through these bags and boxes with her Clits sisters.

She stops. That makes her sad. She didn't even get to say goodbye to either of them. Hell, not to anyone. Not Sophie and Val, barely to Max, not Mouse or Rick or Red or Carla, Gabe, Henry, any of the kids at the Clinic or the Food Bank... Some hero she is, sneaking out of town without a proper farewell. She has addresses, some addresses. And she can send letters for them to post at the Food Bank. Most everyone she cares about will get something she sends there.

She walks back to the rental car, where her brother is now behind the wheel, still humming some little tune. Amy gets into the car, "Ready?" "Yeah, ready. You want Chinese for dinner at the motel?"

She gives him directions back to Lombard with one part of her brain, and slowly, sadly, thinks of everyone she's leaving behind. Larry the Lush, Annie-X, even that bitch Shelly. Amy looks out the window at the City, her Oz, as it flashes by: colorful houses, dirty sidewalks, druggies going about their biz, regular folks doing whatever they do, and each and every one of her friends- even the punks in the scene she doesn't know well at all, out at the Vats, over in Oakland, down in the Valley... She realizes she's going to miss them all. She pauses as the pictures play in her head.

But yeah, that's the point, isn't it? To miss them? And to keep living, to get a move on somewhere, somehow, with her life? Yeah, she can do that. Besides, she thinks maybe she's forgetting the bad stuff, and she needs to remember that too.

She looks over at her brother, navigating the narrow streets and trying not to hit pedestrians as they ignore walk-don't walk instructions. We could be heroes, she thinks, sounds good to me. I wonder what's on KPFA? Or the Quake? That sucks sometimes but sometimes there's decent music, though they never ever play Bowie...

Amy lights up a cigarette and rolls the window down just enough to not fill the car with smoke. She looks at the radio and decides it's not worth even trying. So she peers out the window at the City rolling by and hums a few bars of The Shits' NO MAN'S LAND, yeah that's right.

"San Francisco is 49 square miles surrounded by reality." — **Paul Kantner**

KICK A CAN

1

"We're gonna be late, let's GO." Val urges the loose flock of ambling, grinning punks strewn from one side of the street to the other. "The thing starts at noon, right? What time is it? Isn't it almost one?" She looks around to see who might have a watch. Bags pulls a rusted pocket watch from the inside pocket of his leather jacket and lobs it over to Val.

"Here ya go. Now quit fucking asking us what time it is!" He elicits a couple of giggles from nearby and ducks his head, trying to hide his grin. He likes Val- everyone does- but he's the type of guy who can't let anyone know what he's thinking or feeling. He used to be more easy going, but after the second time he got rolled for every penny in his pockets, he tucked everything down inside and became more aloof. That's who he is today.

Val catches the watch nimbly, plucking it from the air with one quick sweep of her hand. Cradling it in her palm, she inspects it more closely. The glass face is cracked, partly obscuring the hands underneath, though from what Val can see, it is just before one o'clock. Of course, who knows if the thing runs right, has the right time, or is running at all. The second hand is missing too. She holds the watch up to her ear and feels a slight ticking vibration from within.

Ok, so it runs. But still, it's Bag's watch. Who knows what time zone he thinks he's in? Val watches Bags scuff his black army boots along the glistening grey tarmac of the street. It had rained earlier, and everything smells city-fresh: sooty, yet washed clean, just the way Val likes it. She holds up the watch. "Thanks Bags. What a sweetheart."

More giggles from nearby.

Spinning around to walk backwards and face everyone, Val calls out, "Let's pick it up guys. It really is one, and they might be out of food already. And there's no way in hell I'm going over to the fucking Krishna place again. I'm hungry, but not that hungry!" She spins around on her toes again and picks up her pace towards the center of the Panhandle, down Ashbury.

They are headed to one of the free picnics that the soup kitchen puts on in the park every month or so. Sometimes they have a BBQ, sometimes they put out aluminum trays of Chinese food crammed side by side on a row of long tables set end to end. Sometimes there are mounds of cold cuts so you can make a couple of sandwiches- one for now and one for later. Val hopes today is one of those days.

The group straggles across Page through the light traffic, purposely throwing themselves at cars that dare to get in their way. Bags kicks at a silver Audi and sneers, threatening the driver with one raised fist. "Fucking outta my way." He snarls, "We're running LATE."

Looking back, Val smirks. She steps into the street again to get a better peek at the gaggle of punks gathered around the picnic set up mid-park. Sweet! From what Val can glimpse between bodies, it looks like there is still plenty of food laid out across the tables. Whatever it is, Val is hungry. She hasn't eaten anything of substance- some ice cream here, a Life Saver there- in nearly a week. She can feel her ribs easily through her t-shirt and she's feeling a little light-headed.

And she is cold. She's always cold. Unconsciously, she scratches her crotch and walks a little faster, not worrying about the group around her. She needs food, and then to plop down somewhere on the grass to eat it. So what if the picnic is run by hippies? The chow isn't bad, sometimes there's free bread, and if you volunteer, she's heard, you can take home leftovers. Besides, it's a good place to meet up with folks you haven't seen in a while. The last time Val came to one of these, she'd heard about her pal Mitzi, who'd suddenly disappeared the month before. Turns out she'd hitchhiked up the coast with her new guy, that raging skinhead racist asshole Steve-o. Good to hear Mitzi was ok. Sad to hear she was still with that jerk.

She starts jogging a little bit. "Hey guys," she waves one hand distractedly in the air, "See you on the other side. I'm hungry!" As she picks up speed, Val absentmindedly scratches her crotch again and plucks her jeans away from her groin. There's a fierce, persistent itch there- maybe she forgot to change her underwear.

A few of the other gals- all too lean- run to catch up with her. About 10 feet from the row of tables, Val slows down, allowing the other girls to catch up. They leave Val a little room. Sauntering up to the first table, Val squeals as she peers down the length of the laid-out feast. Platters and chafing dishes are still mostly full- they must have had a late start. Looking up, Val notices that folks have just started peeling off to take their plates to sit in groups here and there. Smiling to herself, she sighs and looks forward to a warm meal.

She knows she should take better care of herself. She knows she should eat healthier, or eat more often. There have been times recently, on the trash crew, when she has run out of breath and become dizzy. She's had to sit down and wait for the stars to disappear from twinkling around the edges of her vision. The problem is, Val knows this is all because of the drugs she takes. But she's not about to give them up. She loves getting high and staying high, even enjoys coming down under the right circumstances. If she has enough beer and the right music and her own bed to collapse into.

This is a new dilemma nagging at the back of her brain: continue to get high and let her body continue to break down or stop doing so many drugs and start to take care of herself. She knows one dealer who has started eating healthy foods- organic chocolate milk, salads, fresh fruit- while also cutting back on how often he imbibes in his product. He's a bit of an odd ball, in this community full of odd balls, but there might be something to his new regime... She scratches at her crotch again and waits her turn to step up to the stack of plates.

Bags gets in line behind Val and leans over to see what's being served up today. It looks like a bunch of gloopy salads and some buns and some kind of ground meat in a thick tomato sauce. It doesn't really matter what the hippies cook up. It's food, and it's free. Bags reaches around Val and grabs a paper plate. "Hey! Wait your turn!" She smacks him lightly on the offending arm, and grins. "There's puh-lenty, so..." She grabs the plate from his hands and holds it up in front of her in both hands as a shield. Bags grins, pushes his tongue against the gap between his two front teeth, wags his head, and grabs another plate.

The line moves rather quickly, punks turning their noses up at macaroni salad and unidentifiable greens in a boggy chafing dish. Val looks up from slopping a spoonful of victuals to say thank you to the older grey-dreadlocked hippie in her fuzzy rainbow sweater overseeing the food.

She leans back into Bags, "Eh... what is this, do you think?" Pointing to the chafing dish full of glistening, tomato-ey ground meat. Bags leans over the dish and sniffs. "Goulash?" He looks to the hippie lady, "Hey, what is this?" The older woman looks briefly at the dish and smiles broadly. "That is our famous tofu sloppy joes. Grab a bun and load it up. There are pickles and stuff down there." She points to the end of the tables at a trio of small bowls filled with onion rounds, pickles, and sliced chiles. Bags nods and looks down at Val. "To-Fu. Fucking hippie food." But he grabs the end of the spoon and ladles two large helpings onto his plate, flooding the other large servings of potato salad and slaw on his sagging paper plate.

Val sticks a pinky finger into the slowly spreading mound of sloppy joe on Bags' plate and tentatively places it in her mouth as Bags moves his plate away from her reach. "Hey...

!" Val's eyes widen and she smiles, "Oh my God, that is so good." She plops a spoon-full of fake meat tomato-ey goo onto her plate and moves along. The punkettes behind her follow suit.

At the end of the line, having topped their plates with buns, condiments, and brownies, Val and Bags step away from the tables and start to look around for a good spot to park and eat. The one picnic bench is full, so they glance around at the clusters of punks hunched over their plates to see if there is a circle they should join.

Val gestures with her plate to a tree at the perimeter of the straggling assembly and lifts one eyebrow at Bags. They head that way, careful not to step in any dog shit that might ambush them en route. The punkettes follow, eager to dig in.

Once seated, they each pile the gruel onto buns, and stack onions, pickles and chiles on top of that. Slight groans and lip smacking ensues, this being the one meal in a number of days that most of them have had. Val adjusts her seat and squirms to get comfortable. She takes a bite of food and scratches furiously just to the right of her panty-line. Merde, the itch is starting to catch fire. What is going on down there?

Bags can't help but notice. "Fire in the hole?" He grins at his own joke. Val presses her lips together and frowns slightly. "I don't know what's going on. My cooter is on fire." She blushes slightly, though really, this is Bags she's talking to. No need to be shy. One of the punkettes- Val can't remember which is which from this group- pauses mid-bite. "Is it burning in more than one spot?" Val scratches again and nods, yup. The punkette shoves her lower lip out in empathy. "You might want to hit the clinic. I had that too. Well, have it. You might have Herpes, Val. It's sorta going around."

Scratching again, Val blurts out, "What the fuck?" One of the other punkettes- the one with a rash of speed scabs across the bridge of her nose- folds her now empty plate in half and puts it aside. "Me too. I got it from Buck before he was with Kelly-Belly. She has to have it too." She turns to punkette #1, "Did you fuck Buck too?"

Punkette #1 shakes her head no. "No I got it from Paulie." She looks at Val, "Who you been doing lately?" Val puts her half-full plate of food down on the patchy grass in front of her. Fuck. She'd slept with Paulie last month, just a one-time thing while they were hanging out one night, high on heroin, and nothing else going on. "I slept with Paulie last month. Shouldn't I have felt something before now?" And then she sighs. "Merde. I did have some kind of little bumps and it hurt a little, there, after that. But I figured I just needed to wash myself better, and after a couple of days, it went away." She scrunches her mouth into a moue. "Fuck."

Punkette #1 cracks her knuckles. "That could still be Herpes. You could be a carrier. I think that's how that works. I think you can feel it, not feel it, whatever. But then it will come and go. I don't know. I don't understand exactly how that works. You should go to the clinic, though. Sounds like we all got the same crap. Clap. Hah."

Bags has been silently taking this in, gazing at other groups around them as the punkettes talk and finishing the food on his plate. He speaks up. "Yeah... Mitzi gave it to me. Wasn't she hanging with Paulie for a while? It fucking burns, man." He leans his leather-clad elbow on one knee. "You just gotta keep it clean and get through it."

Val looks around at Bags, punkettes #1 and 2, and the others. "So... you all have Herpes?" One punkette pipes up, "Not me. But I'm a virgin, so..." Val looks around at the other rag-tag collection of punks finishing up their meals and at the line of folks- many of whom she knows- in the line. "I wonder how many of us have this? Except for you." She points to the virgin punkette, "Are we just passing it around?" The punkettes all nod and look around, each trying to determine who might have herpes and who is passing it on.

Bags snuffles as he crumples up his soggy paper plate and tosses it at a mohawk sitting in another group nearby. "So, anyone going to the East Bay gig tomorrow?" The punkettes' eyes all brighten and they pipe in at once, "Yeah!" "I'm going with that hippie dude from the light show company!" "We have a ride!"

Punkette #1 offers, "That Brotherhood of Light guy, Ed, and his old lady Stine." She gestures around at the other punkettes. "We were over there last week, scoring some speed. We were there for hours, waiting for this biker guy to show up. And Steph there," she points to the girl with all the scabs across her nose, "started looking at all this gear that was all over the place. All these screens and projectors and other stuff."

Steph jumps in, "I did AV in high school, so I knew what some of that gear was. That guy Ed owns the company. He showed me some really cool shit." She talks faster, excited to share what she knows. "You put layers of all these oils on the overhead projector bed and swirl them around. They don't blend together. They make bubbles and swirly shapes, all that LSD looking stuff. It's actually kinda cool. He asked if I wanted to come help him set up the show.

There's all these screens to erect, and the oils to prepare, and the whole electric lay out. I think it will be fun."

Val scratches at her panty-line and nods her head, "Cooooool! That does sound like fun."

She looks at Bags. "Are you going?" Bags nods, "Yup. A bunch of us are taking BART to Oakland and the train up to whatever that stop is closest to the Aquatic Park, then it's not too far to walk. Want to join? We should head out around 11:30. Show starts at twelve but..."

Steph interrupts him, "No, show starts at eleven."

Bags quips, "Yeah but I don't need to be there to watch a bunch of Hell's Angels stand around and scratch their asses. Show won't really start 'til after twelve, so..." He shrugs. Punkette #1 leans over and bumps Bags with her shoulder, "We can come, right, Tee?" She looks at punkette #3. Tee bobs her head up and down, "Sounds good. Should we meet up in the Mission or...?"

Val suggests, "Why not meet up at our place? We can all head to 16th and jump BART there." The punkettes trade smiles. For Val to invite them to meet up with her, that's large. Punkette #1 and Tee both squeak "Sure!" at the same time. Bags snorts, "Why not?"

Steph pulls the one limp cigarette she has tucked behind her ear and tries to light it up off the almost empty blue Bic lighter from her pocket. It catches on the 3rd try. She shakes the lighter and deciding it's toast, tucks it into the small pile of folded, discarded paper plates. "I have to go mega early to meet Ed, so I'll see you guys there."

Val stands and scratches her crotch. "I'm heading over to the clinic. This is getting bad." Bags and the punkettes all nod in agreement. Bags stands too, his leather creaking as he stretches his arms over his head. "I'll come with you."

Val bends down and picks up her unfinished plate of food. She glances over to the line of tables, looking for the trash barrel that is usually parked at one end. Not there. She looks around, and seeing the park trash can, heads in that direction. Steph or Tee- now Val can't remember again- scoops up everyone's discarded paper plates and joins her. "You gonna finish that?" She points to the half-eaten hamburger seeping tofu sloppy joe and pickles. "Nope. You want it?" Val offers the punkette the grease-stained plate. The punkette jogs to the trash and lobs in her two handfuls of debris, then skips back to Val and takes the proffered plate. Folding it in half, she crimps the edges over and tucks it, oozing, into her jacket pocket. There will be tofu muck there for weeks to come.

"Thanks. I'm gonna hang, go for a skate with my girls."
Tee looks up into Val's face– she is easily five inches shorter
than the respected Quebecoise punk. "Good luck with your
cootch." Val pouts a little in mock reply and says "Thanks.
See you all tomorrow, oueeh?" Tee gives two thumbs up
and skips backwards to the other punkettes. Bags joins Val,
and they make their way out of the park, back towards the
Haight/Clayton corner where the free clinic sits nestled
between funky hippie shops and the post office.

2

As they saunter across Oak onto Ashbury, towards Haight where they will turn right on Clayton, Val scratches and pulls her pants away from her crotch again. "Fuck, this really hurts now. Thanks for coming with me." Bags kicks an empty dog food can lying on the sidewalk. "Sure, don't got nothing else to do..." He crosses in front of Val and kicks at the can again. Val sweeps her foot out and stops the can in its trajectory, places her toe just over the top of the can, nudging it backwards, then kicks it down the sidewalk with a strong 'pop'! Bags laughs and runs to catch the can, tripping a little over his ratty greying Doc Martens.

He kicks the can back to Val, who, even though her pussy feels like it's being jabbed in multiple spots with a sharp pick, plays along. She sidesteps twice to catch the wobbling can between her two feet, dribbles it back and forth, and kicks it further down the street again. Bags dutifully chases it down. "Good boy," thinks Val, smiling to herself.

They kick the can all the way down to Clayton, where Bags promptly flattens it by stomping on it twice. He kicks the crumpled can so it bounces off the wall and comes to a stop by the needle bin parked off to the side of the clinic's front door. Val starts to head up the few stairs inside, stops and turns. "You don't have to come inside. I'm a big girl." Bags waves her inside. "Nah, seriously, I don't got nothing else to do. 'Sides, after they check you out, maybe we can head over to Annie X's and see what's new? I hear there's some sweet, clean shit going around... Uh, I think I'll go grab a Pepsi at the Blue Unicorn first. You want anything?"

"Annie's sounds good to me. And ooo I'm thirsty. Can you get me a Pepsi too?" She reaches into the orange and green plaid flannel pouch that hangs off her 2" leather studded belt. "I have some money..." Bags leans against the gateway at the bottom of the stairs. His only income these days is from whatever junk he finds on the street and sells. Hippies throw away a lot of good shit. Once or twice a week, he lays all his scavenged goods out neatly along the sidewalk at the corner of Baker and Haight, sells what he can, and dumps the rest. There have been days where he's walked away with a good score of a few hundred bucks. Stupid hippies.

Right now though, he only has enough to buy some speed and a few bucks left over for a Pepsi and the train out to the show tomorrow. He knows he can get a free meal whenever he's hungry again, and there's usually free beer at Pat's or wherever he lands. Since he never looks beyond the next couple of days, he's set for now, but not flush. Val counts out a few dollars into Bags' hand, and clomps up the stairs until she pushes open the door and heads inside. "Thanks!" She yells over her shoulder.

Bags shoves his hands deep into his front jeans pockets and moseys up Clayton to Frederick Street and the coffee house. He's not in any hurry. He squints a little in the early afternoon sun that has appeared overhead. He lost his shades– a week ago? Two weeks ago? He has no idea of time passing. He has here and now, and 'then' hazily floating around in his head. But nothing that concretely tethers a specific timeline with events marching along one after the other.

He shrugs off the thought. That's what speed does to you– rolls all your hours into one spaghetti bundle. You can pick out 'oh this happened' but you can't pinpoint exactly when or sometimes where or who with... And even then, sometimes what he remembers isn't exactly what happened at all. There was that one time he was sure there were teeny tiny FBI agents hiding in the bushes and trees as he made his way across the Haight from his dealer's place to wherever he called home at the time. They whispered ferociously and Bags was sure they were following him... Now, of course, he knows that was the speed and how many days he had gone without sleep that caused him to hallucinate. So, ok, most of the time he can remember real stuff that has happened. He fingers the hole in his right pocket and wishes he hadn't flattened that can so he could kick it all the way to the Blue Unicorn and back again.

There is only one other person at the clinic so Val is quickly ushered into a room where she is asked to remove her lower garments and drape a paper sheet over her lap. The doc is a lady with frizzy grey hair pulled back into a tightly wound bun at the base of her neck. She reminds Val of her auntie back home, so Val feels safe and comfortable under her gaze. She places her feet awkwardly in the stirrups and the doc pokes around her cootch, where she scrapes one of the burning spots so that it feels like it's bleeding now too. The doc tells Val to get dressed and she'll be right back.

As Val is tightening the laces on her left boot, the doc returns and says, "Ms. Croteau, you do indeed have an STD: Herpes. We have a lab right here to test for viral cultures, since so many of our patients have no fixed addresses. Otherwise, you would have had to wait a week for your results." She hands Val a few sheets of stapled paper, one of which has the heading Herpes- What Do I Do Next? Val glances at the columns of print below the heading, but the doc says, "This is for your reference. First off, you should contact and inform all your recent sexual partners."

Val snorts, "Phuh... only one, and I know he gave it to me cause he gave it to someone else I know too." She hunches down and waits for the doc to say something more. She thinks, 'This sucks', and finishes tying her boots.

The doc continues, "Well... you are not alone, even in that. Up to 80% of Americans have Herpes..." She holds up her hand. "I know, you are Canadian." The doc smiles. "But you still count in that number. The burning you are feeling is coming from cold sores you have around the inner labia of your vagina. These will break and ooze before healing up, which can last between seven to ten days. It is very important to keep the area clean and dry so the sores don't spread during this outbreak." She pauses. "Once these have healed though, that doesn't mean you are cured. Once you have Herpes, you will always have Herpes."

Val groans. "Merde... is there nothing we can do?"

"No, I am sorry Ms. Croteau. All we can do is give you something to help alleviate the discomfort, and to speed up the healing process. But nothing to make it go away forever. I'm going to prescribe an ointment to help alleviate your symptoms, and an antibiotic to help reign in the outbreak. Sandra up front will process these scrips for you. Meanwhile, I suggest that you follow the instructions on these pamphlets I gave you."

She smiles faintly at Val. "To ease the burning you're feeling, press a bag of frozen peas up against your genitals- against your underwear, that is. Or wrap some ice in a clean cloth. Please keep the area very clean. Wash yourself, but do not touch with your fingers, as you may spread the sores to another part of your vagina. Wear cotton underwear and loose fitting pants or skirts to keep the area from becoming too warm or wet."

Val thinks, 'I'm not planning to get wet there for a long, long time.' "Chuh!"

"Also, if you are able, take a warm bath to open up the sores. That helps move the healing process along. Be sure to dry the area thoroughly after, just... patting the sores dry. And the last thing, for future reference..." the doc leans against the counter behind her. "If you can avoid triggers that cause new outbreaks, please do. Don't have sex while you have an outbreak, or even think you feel one coming on. There are symptoms that you will come to recognize. Small bumps that will appear on your genitalia, a tingling sensation, and then the burning and itching that you are experiencing now. If you have one sexual partner- or multiple- and continue to be sexually active- please have them wear a condom. Or wait until the scabs have fallen off before having intercourse. Wash your hands often. Most importantly is to both avoid passing this on to others, and to try to avoid triggering outbreaks again."

Val rolls her shoulders and tilts her head to one side. That's a lot to remember, and her cooter is still burning. "How do I avoid triggering this outbreak?"

"The best thing you can do is to avoid stress." The doc shrugs. "I know that for a lot of you kids out there on the streets, that is a tough order to follow. The City can be stressful all on its own, and all the stories I hear... kids living on the streets, in dumpsters, in squats with no electricity or heat, no hot water... plus I know not a lot of you are eating regularly. And you're stressing your bodies with whatever drugs you are taking." She pauses. "I don't need to tell you, I know. Just please try to be better to yourself. Do you have a warm, dry place to sleep at night?"

Val nods. "Yes. I live just on the other side of the panhandle. In an apartment. We have heat, electricity, hot water, all that stuff."

The doc smiles and crosses her arms. "Ok, good. Mm, and I have to tell you, I think you are severely underweight. If you are able to eat more regularly, take care of yourself a bit better, that should help keep outbreaks at bay. I can't help but notice your track marks." The doc reaches into the drawer behind her and brings out a folded pamphlet. "Not to push, but if you are interested, you could check this out." She hands Val a khaki pamphlet that reads Who, What, How and Why across the top. Val snorts again.

"Thanks doc. I'm not interested in that 12-step bullshit. God and all that." She pauses, "... but I have been thinking about eating better." Val points in the general direction where Marco, the dealer she knows who has been eating healthy meals, lives. "I have a friend who has been eating organic salads and yoghurt. Just eating healthy. I can do what he's been doing and take better care of myself. But that..." she hands the pamphlet back to the doc, "Nope."

The doc places the pamphlet back into the drawer and holds her hands up in a gesture of defeat. "Hey, win some, lose some. I pick my battles, and if I can help you stave off another outbreak, and not pass this STD along, and get you eating better? That's three out of four, and an excellent start." She turns and opens the door as Val rolls the stapled sheets up and shoves them into her back pocket.

"Thanks for not giving me a sermon, doc." Val wonders, or did she? She doesn't think so. She'll swing by Marco's place after she and Bags hit Annie's. That feels like a step in the right direction. Something on her own, for herself, and not as part of the squad, which she normally loves. This feels very personal and very private though. She'll keep these ideas to herself for now. Who knows? Maybe she can get Sophie to come along for the ride too. It makes sense to Val that she should be able to eat well and continue to shoot speed. She should be able to keep living the life and just change that one thing.

Val exits the exam room and walks up to the front desk, where Sandra fills the prescriptions for her. Val never thought about it before– that the clinic is also a pharmacy. But of course. She knows punks who have picked up scrips of Methadone and other stuff here. Luckily, she thinks, Val has never liked heroin or any of the pills that make you feel that way. She likes to go fast, go hard, get intense, and heroin and all that shit doesn't go that way. Yeah... she's not going to stop doing speed!

As Val finishes paying for the two prescriptions and shoves them into her flannel pouch, Bags pushes the front door open with his shoulder, trying not to spill the two drinks in his hands.

"Perfect timing. I'm all done here." Val reaches for her drink. Bags relinquishes the cold plastic cup and dries his fingers on his jeans. She jiggles the straw around in the cup and takes a long, satisfying suck. She is so thirsty. She squares her shoulders, "You ready to go to Annie's? She should be up by now." Bags takes a glug of his Pepsi. "Let's hit it."

They trip down the stairs in their thick, heavy boots, look

up and down Clayton to see who they might know, and make their way back across the panhandle towards Annie X's.

Val remembers, "Shit, I don't have a rig with me. Do you…?" Bags thinks, visualizing what's in his jacket pockets, and says, "Nope. I heard Annie picked up a whole box from somewhere though, so if you don't mind shelling out for it, we can buy a fresh spike off her."

Val looks impressed. "How did she do that? They're all brand new?"

Bags tries to recall who told him. He vaguely remembers leaning against a wall somewhere and someone leaning next to him talking about Annie's latest batch and other goodies. "I heard someone stole them from a pharmacy… or she has a connect at one, something like that. But yeah, brand new box. The last rig I shared with Paulie a few days ago was so dull, we even tried to sharpen it on a whetstone."

"Did that work?"

"Nah, it actually made the needle a little, kinda…barbed? Like it went in ok, but coming out seemed to stick with these little spiky bits. We both shot up any way, but that rig got tossed." He mimes tossing something away.

As they cross into the park, Val takes another long guzzle of her drink. She sips more, freezing her tongue, though she doesn't mind too much. Her feet are cold, her ears are cold, and her tongue is a little frozen. Great. A fresh hit of speed will even all that out.

Val and Bags shuffle quietly across the park down to Lyon, where they cross the street and make their way up towards Fulton. Hopefully Annie X is open for business. Bags crushes his now empty cup and tosses it into a straggly bush growing up against one of the houses they pass. He shrugs the collar of his leather off his neck in anticipation of the heat that is coming.

They reach Annie X' building. She doesn't like anyone to use the bell, and since neither thought to page her, their only option is to yell at the upstairs windows from the street. They both pause and look at one another. "You want me...?" Bags places both hands around his mouth and shouts up, "Hey Annie! You in?" They wait, shuffle their feet, looking around to see if they are bothering anyone. Bags tries again, a little louder, "Annie! X!"

He is about to yell up one more time, when the window thuds open above them. They step back and see a mop of bright, candy apple red hair poke out. It's Babs, Annie X' current roommate, with a newly dyed 'do.

Even though neither of them pays rent in this squat, Annie has been known to enforce homage rent- that is, whatever someone else owns that Annie covets is paid to her so they can stay there too. After all, Annie is the one who cut the locks on the electric box so they could have electricity.

3

Babs waves at them. "She's in the shower! But you can come up and wait. Be right down!" She pulls her head back inside and a moment later, Bags and Val hear her flurry of light footsteps tumbling down the stairs to the front door. The door flings open and Babs gushes, "Hey! Good to see you both! What's going on?! Come on in! Annie should be right out..." She turns and heads back upstairs, motioning for them to follow, which they do. She talks over her shoulder at them the entire time. There is a good reason she is called Babs. She is constantly babbling, especially when high. Though Val isn't listening, the stream of words feeds her anticipation. This batch must be good...

Babs turns at the top of the stairwell into the front room, which is furnished rather carefully with what Annie deems to be appropriate parlor furniture. There are narrow tables on spindly legs, a couple of slightly grungy but fairly clean overstuffed nubby chairs on short, ornate feet. There is a faded and threadbare Persian rug. Every surface has at least one Marilyn Monroe memento atop it- framed photos, ashtrays, coasters. And as old as everything is, the corners of the room and everything in it are spotless. Speed cleaning at its best.

Babs plops herself down on the floor by the stereo and looks up at the other two. "She should be right out. How you doing? What's going on?" She picks at the peeling polish on her toenails, shredding small pieces into a pile at her feet.

Val takes a sip of her cider. "Just you know, here for a little business." She sits in a faded salmon colored chair. With her back to the wall, she can turn her head and see out the front bay windows, and turning her head the other way, she can see the whole room plus part of the small hall that leads to the empty kitchen. She pulls at the crotch of her pants and scratches herself distractedly.

Bags walks to the bay windows and checks out the Marilyn paraphernalia along the sills: small figurines, a bobble-head Marilyn, more ashtrays. He leans one arm on the window frame and looks down the street. "You going to the Berkeley show tomorrow night?"

Babs hugs her arms to her sides and grins hugely, "Yes! I love the Lewd! I'm not sure how to get there... where is it?"

Val scratches and sighs. "Aquatic Park in Berkeley. Right next to the railroad tracks along the water. Should be a good show. Um, Wasted Youth, JFA, a bunch of good bands are playing. Should be a good show." She pauses, "Oh, I just said that."

Babs giggles. "So... BART to where?" She looks at Val, then Bags, then back to Val again. Her eyes are vibrating, she's so high.

Bags seems distracted by something out on the street, so Val replies. "There's a bunch of us taking BART from the Mission at noon. You go to West Oakland, then switch to the Oaky BART at the UC Campus. You get off, I don't know... 20 stops? Then there's a little hike, or skate, about a mile to the park."

Bags grumbles, "Meh it's not far. Quick mile, yeah." His brain has shut down a little, this close to scoring, being forced to wait. Val snort-laughs and turns her attention to Babs, who is starting to get under her skin. If she were high, maybe not so much. But unfairly, Babs is high and Val is cold, and oh-so ready for her first shot of the day. Plus there's the damned itching and burning. She needs to get high, shower, change, put some of that ointment on her cootch, and go see Marco. Then maybe do some painting. She can't think that far ahead though. Just... first score, and whatever else comes next.

"Well, can I come? Who else is going? Are you meeting at the 16th street BART?" She starts rocking back and forth, hugging her knees to her chest, bouncing from the tips of her toes, shove back, forward, back. Val closes her eyes and sighs again. "Sure. Meet at my place at 11:30. We can catch the 33 down to Market and walk up. Then off to Berkeley we go."

The pocket doors behind Babs rumble open, and Annie, hair wrapped in a terry cloth towel, her lime green vintage quilted smoking jacket, and full Marilyn make-up, steps into the room. "Hidey ho, all. Val, Bags." She reaches into her pocket for a cigarette and comes up empty handed. "Crap. Babs, go get me some cigs. Here's some money." She reaches over to a table just inside her boudoir and drops a fiver into Babs' lap. "Jasmine Sobranies, 'k?"

Babs jumps up and runs back through the kitchen to her room. She runs back out, horsehide lace-up boots in hand. Sitting at the top of the stairs, she quickly pulls her boots on, laces them up, and tromps downstairs and out the door. She calls out "Gotchya! I'll be right back!" and something else as the door shuts behind her.

Val rolls her eyes and looks at Annie. "How do you deal with that?"

Annie shakes her head and purses her lips. "I tune her out most of the time. And usually I make her leave. So..." She shrugs. "I got some great records out of the deal." She points to the stack of vinyl leaning up against the stereo on its crates, where Babs had been sitting. "Older shit, but classics."

Bags walks over and starts flipping through the stack. The Tubes, Blondie, Ian Dury, Sex Pistols. Sure, obvious 'punk starter' record collection. He looks up to Annie. "Can I...?" She nods, "Sure. Just not too loud. And no Bauhaus. That's all Babs plays..."

He decides on The Clash, pulls the record carefully out of its sleeve and onto side one on the turntable. Click on, lift the stylus and place it on the record, check that the speed is set to 33 rpm. The first bomp bomp bomp beats of London Calling fill the room, and Bags adjusts the sound a little louder. He looks to Annie to make sure it's ok, but she has already disappeared into her boudoir. She doesn't say anything, so it must be fine.

Val rocks her head in time with the song, and pulls, then scratches at her crotch. "Hey Annie! Do you mind if I use your bathroom before we get started?" She needs to put some ointment on now, if that will help at all. Annie calls back, "Sure! I'll set up out front!" And with that, Val jumps to her feet and walks quickly through the small kitchen to the smaller bath off to its side.

Annie carefully carries a small ornate table inlaid with

mother of pearl atop criss-crossed carved wooden legs into the front room. She sets the table down, and heads back into her room, emerging a moment later with a pale blue, plump round leather footrest. She sets this behind the small table and lowers her bulk onto the footrest. Arranged around the table are a scale, a small baggie of sparkling crystals, and a snuffbox filled with smaller cellophane baggies, empty and awaiting measured goods. There is also a brand-new box of needles. Bags' shoulders cramp slightly at the thought of what's coming next. He cracks his neck and sits in the salmon chair Val just vacated.

"So. What's your pleasure? I got this amazing batch from my new connect. You won't believe how clean this is." She gestures to the blue and white box of needles. "And these... brand new, if you need one." Bags leans in and rubs his hands together. "Yup, quarter bag for me. Not sure what Val wants. I think she's getting a rig too."

Annie starts to set up the scale. "Ok, I'll take care of you first. The quarter costs thirty dollars for this shit. Cool?"

Bags frowns slightly. "Uh I only have twenty-five. Can you short me whatever? Or I can owe you?" His stomach starts to churn, all that hippie grub moving around on what had been an empty stomach.

Annie pauses with the full baggie poised over the scale. "No can do. Thirty dollars or a dime bag." She raises one eyebrow, what's it gonna be?

Val comes out of the bathroom, "I can loan you the five bucks Bags. I know you're good for it. Eventually, anyway." She grins. "And uh, what's a half? Fifty?"

Bags dips his head as thanks and wipes his hands on his knees. Annie starts to weigh out Bag's purchase. Fifty-five dollars, my dear Val. And since you're so cute, I'll throw in a spike." She looks up at Val to make sure her meaning got through. Val smiles, "Thank you, do me a half." She walks over to the window and looks down at the street, then turns and sits in the low sun-faded turquoise loveseat partly blocking the window. She clears her throat and lightly touches her crotch. The ointment has had a cooling effect, but everything still itches like crazy.

Annie evenly measures out Bags' quarter, swiftly pouring the stuff into a clean cellophane baggie, and methodically folds it and begins to tape it up. Bags shuffles his feet, "Don't close it up. We were gonna do some here?" To which Annie replies, "Nope, sorry. I'm offering tastes if anyone needs that, but this isn't a shooting gallery anymore. Mostly, I don't want to encourage-" as the downstairs door opens and Babs comes clipping up the stairs, "Hey! I'm back! I got your cigs, and some Red Hots too, if anyone wants any?!" She waves the box around the room and holds the Sobranies out to Annie. "That." Annie finishes. She takes the proffered cigarettes and drops them in her smoking jacket pocket, then finishes taping the baggie shut.

Bags stands and pulls out the wadded bills from his left front pocket. He smooths the bills out, counting 1-3-5-10-20-25. Val reaches into her flannel pouch and brings out one of the small flannel wallets she and Kelly-Belly had sewn and sold at shows a few months ago. She extracts three twenties, and hands them to Annie. Bags places his money on top of Val's. Annie quickly thumbs through the bills, drops them in her pocket, and pops her neck to the left and right. Val cringes. She hates the sound of joints cracking. It just gives her the creeps. Like some people don't like the sound of nails on the chalkboard. Val's never minded that. But clowns and joints popping, merci, non.

Annie hands Bags his baggie and turns her attention back to the scale. Babs turns the record over and plays the other side as Annie weighs out Val's goods. Once weighed, poured, rolled and taped, Annie opens the box of needles, gingerly chooses one, and hands both the needle and baggie to Val. She carefully closes up her stash, locks the scale back down, and with difficulty, heaves herself off the footstool and to her feet. As Bags and Val tap their drugs and put them away, moving quickly in anticipation of shooting up elsewhere, Annie returns the table to her boudoir- still unlit and shadowy- then the footstool as well.

"Alright?! We good here? I have an appointment I need to finish getting ready for." She sweeps one hand towards the door to move them along.

Bags and Val say "Yup" "Good here" and head for the stairs. Babs pipes up, "So I'll see you tomorrow at 11:30 at 16th Street?!"

Val pauses at the top of the stairs as Bags stomps down hurriedly. "No... my place. 11:30. Then we take the bus. Or you can meet us in the Mission if you like. Or the show." She starts down the stairs as Babs replies behind her "Ok! Great! Your place! See you then!" Annie shuts the pocket doors to her boudoir and Babs is left at the top of the stairs, wondering who to talk to now.

"East is East, and West is San Francisco." **O. Henry**

Jump the Train

1

Val closes the blanket drawn across the window in her room to shut out the bright daylight outside. Her eyes are jittery, jumping back and forth, which gives her a small headache and makes her stomach flip flop. The darkened room relaxes her eyes, so she turns from the window and considers which t-shirt to wear, which shoes. Will she skate and wear her hi-tops? Or mosh and wear her combat boots? She decides on the pit, which also dictates which shirt. Her fave tee already has a tear across the back of the neck, and she doesn't want to risk it being torn further by what will most certainly be an aggressive pit today.

She rummages through her shirts and decides on her Husker Dü tee and a slightly crusty black hoodie, topping that off with an armless, fraying red plaid flannel. She dabs a little ointment onto the spots in her cootch and wipes her hand off on the flannel vest. She pulls on clean underwear and slightly dirty black Levis and sits on her rumpled bed to finish up with fresh socks and the combat boots.

For a finishing touch, Val wraps a couple of spiked and

studded black leather belts around her waist, and the four spiked leather wrist bands she always wears– two wide and two narrow– one of each on each wrist. She snaps those in place atop the miscellaneous bits of leather, cloth, and string that she's constantly replacing as they break. It's one of her tweaker things. She likes how it feels when she skates fast and tough and the little bits of string and cloth flutter along her wrists.

Val checks the flannel pouch hanging from her belt. She has a little cash, some change from panhandling last night with Bags, and her ID. She grabs her cheap, fake aviator glasses, looks around the dark room, and decides she's ready to go. She can hear Sophie arguing with Henry in her room next door. Not what they are saying, just the tone in their voices. Though maybe that's romance talk for those two. Val shakes her head and smiles. She'll never understand Sophie, as much as she loves her as a pal. She already misses Doucie– Amy– though it's only been a few days since she split town with her brother. Back to that Podunk town in Canada, pourquoi?! Meh, she shrugs… Amy'll be back.

Meanwhile, she checks her money and ID again, and thinks– ointment applied, paints put away, sunglasses in hand. Val stayed up all night with Bags so her thoughts are bouncing all over the place. They came back to Pat's place after leaving Annie X's, filled a jelly jar with water from the bathroom and shut Val's bedroom door on the catcalls from Sophie, Henry and Max in the other room. "Ooooooooooo" "Get it!" "Go, Bags!"

They took turns shooting up with the brand-new rig. Val went first since she paid for it. The speed was sparkly and cold. This is Val's favorite kind of high. Everything is concise, with sharp, clean corners, and a searing, almost antiseptic aftertaste. She tries to work up a little spit to get at the dregs of that taste at the back of her throat. She eeks out a bit more of the cold, clean flavor as she opens her bedroom door and gasps. Bags is looming against the wall right outside her door with a crooked grin on his face.

"Hey! I wasn't sure if I should rap on your door or what!" His face is gaunt after their all-night bender. They'd shot up and talked for a while as Val brought out her paints and tried to do a portrait of Bags. She isn't good with faces though, so the constant dabbing and smudging only made him look like a bleary clown. Val finally gave up and turned the painting towards the wall. It would watch her otherwise...

They'd headed out to the street, Bags borrowing Gabe's board, and skated down to Divisadero and the Lower Haight, where they panhandled half-heartedly for a while,

shared a lemonade, and skated over to the Castro for some good old-fashioned gay taunting. They tried to out-do each other, hurling technicolor insults and spitting at a few more flamboyant types, until they got bored.

They returned to Pat's just before dawn, where Val pulled a fresh flat canvas from behind her dresser and started in on a new painting- something starry and jagged. Bags folded himself up into a corner of Val's room and drew tiny, frantic cartoons that filled every page. None of it made any sense, but he couldn't stop, pressing down into the paper so hard it tore. He began covering old cartoons with new drawings, a jumble of dark black lines scribbled all over each page. At the time, he was sure he was creating a masterpiece. Later, Val threw the pages away.

As Val's eyes began to jitter, Bags decided to take a bath. Val was on the precipice of still feeling high and coming down, so she didn't know where he'd gone, only that she was suddenly alone in her room. She'd stripped down and tried to paint some more, then pulled her curtain back to a startlingly bright wash of sunshine that ended her painting spree.

And now, here's Bags, looking as broken and done in by the long night as she feels. They're going to need another shot, and maybe something cold and sweet. Ice cream is made with milk, she thinks. That's healthy, right? "Ya wanna wake up?" She gestures to her room. Bags grins and pushes off from the wall. "Exactly what I was thinking."

As Val sets everything up for her shot, Bags toys with the shades he found under the couch in the kitchen. They're made of heavy plastic square rims and dark tinted glass. One of the arms is bent, and he worries at it, trying to fix the piece so he can have some kind of respite in all that right light ouside. He can tell it's going to be a hot, uncomfortable day. He might even stash his leather here in Val's room so he doesn't melt into a huge, stanky puddle of speed sweat at the show.

They each shoot up in turn, Bags' stash down to one last remaining hit. That's enough to pick him up again later today or start over tomorrow. He realizes he'll have to borrow someone's rig if he's going to shoot up at the show, though he can't think where he would do that. He visited the park where the show is being held a few weeks back, doing a little recon. He wanted to see where the stage would be and if there was a way in and out in case of emergency. You never know with these outdoor shows' security-run by the Angels. Shit has been known to go bad before, and Bags likes to watch his own back.

While Bags fidgets with his jacket, pulling out change,

gum and an old Muni pass that he hopes still works, Val splashes some water on her face in the bathroom, and rubs a hand over the week-old stubble on top of her head. Time for a shave, but not today. She flicks beads of water off her fringe, and steps into the kitchen at the same time that Max emerges from Amy's old room. He has been crashing there since she left, more out of convenience than romance. She's gone, there's a spare bed. No one minds if he practices drum bits in that back room, so for now, it's where he ends up every night.

Val opens the freezer door and squeals as she pulls out an almost empty carton of Double Rainbow Caramel. She tucks the lid into the greasy pile of dishes on the counter and sticks her finger into the bottom of the carton. C'est parfait, that's exactly what she wanted. The sugar pairs perfectly with the speed. Val feels ready for the day now.

Max has a fresh buzz on his scalp, and sports a clean wife-beater, passably clean Levis, and cracked leather boots. His stick bag hangs off one shoulder, and he has a stack of cymbals tucked under his other arm. He wishes he could afford a cymbal bag, but there's no dough for that sort of luxury.

"Is Henry up yet? We gotta bolt, man."

Val tilts her head over one shoulder towards the front of the apartment. "I heard him and Sophie going at it a little while ago. So yeah he's up, but I haven't seen him."

Max peers into the ice cream container, sees that it's empty, and makes his way to Sophie and Henry's room. Banging on the door, he yells, "Let's move it!" Bang bang bang. "Henry!"

Henry slams the door open so that it cracks hard against the dresser that blocks it from opening all the way. "Fucking fuck, Max." He growls. I'm fucking ready. Where's Gabe?"

"He's parking the van out front. Let's go." Max gets nervous for these bigger shows. He's fine on their home turf, The Tool and Die, and the various out of town shows they've played at tiny bars and garages all around the Bay Area. They opened once for The Avengers at Mabuhay Gardens, and he was a mess before that show. Once they start playing, he mellows out. But the idea of so many faces he doesn't know all that well wrecks him before he hits the stage. Henry doesn't do well with nervous nellies. It brings out the Sarge in him.

"Relax, junior. Lemme piss and I'll be right out."

Val and Bags make room for Henry to pass. He's fuming, and the anger comes off his clenched fists in visible waves. Val salutes Sophie with a wave of the ice cream container. "Hey Soph. You coming with us or riding with?" Sophie hangs off the doorjamb of her room with both arms. "I'll come with you. Henry's pissing me off right now." She glances at the closed bathroom door. "I'll tell you outside."

Max says hi to Sophie and clomps down the stairs. He's not angry, but the sound of his boots hitting the boards makes it sound like he is. "Tell Henry I'm out front," he yells, as he shifts cymbals to get through the door outside.

Val tosses the empty ice cream carton in the general direction of the overflowing trash bin, checks her flannel pouch one more time for money, ID, works. "Let's go wait outside for Tee and all them." Bags follows her to the top of the stairs, where she pauses and waits for Sophie to grab her hoodie. Sophie's wearing a new Nuns t shirt she stole from that tourist-punk store up on Haight. Any chance they can get to nab stuff from that place, they do. No one has been caught yet, so they keep going back for more. Amy had stolen a whole box of great charm-like miniature silver crosses, pistols, scissors, and knives. All three of them wore a mish-mash of these from hoops in their ears and on their jackets until they lost them somewhere. Val still has one small jackknife precariously hanging off a thin leather strap around one wrist.

Sophie looks around her room, shuts the door, and clicks the lock into place. They've all learned to lock their doors from Pat's prying eyes and thieving hands. "Let's go."

Val allows Sophie the lead, then follows, Bags giving them space as he takes up the rear. Sophie punches the door open, and quickly covers her eyes in the bright morning sun. She fumbles for her rose tinted wire-rimmed shades as Val and Bags emerge into daylight, hissing and grinding their teeth, vampiric. Bags whines, "What is that thing in the sky?" They have been up for too long, it's too bright. On go sunglasses, oh what happened to their beloved fog? They sit on the stairs and wait for Gabe to show up with the van, and the punkettes and whoever else they had invited to join the rest of them.

Val closes her eyes behind her mirrored shades. She tilts her head back and allows the sun to wash over her face and neck. That feels alright, she supposes. If it wasn't so bright, at least she's warm for the first time in months. With her eyes scrunched up, she tunes in on the sounds around her. Max grumbling to himself one door down, tap tap tapping his fingers on trash bins and a nearby car. She can tell he's nervous about the show. A plane flying overhead. Birds in the eaves of the houses around them. Sophie lighting up a cig, inhaling, and blowing out sweet tobacco smoke. Voices turning the corner, giggles, brash and melodic at once. Punks on a mission. She opens her eyes and squints up the street to see Tee, Steph and the other punkette whose name she will never remember marching up the sidewalk in a tight gaggle, all cut-off sleeves, freshly shaved heads, and jangling studded leather belts.

They skirt around Max, a little in awe- he's right there! Tee waves to Val and the punkettes arrange themselves in calculated postures- hands firmly tucked into back pockets, or leaning against the stair rail, or one arm wrapped around the other in a rubbery twist of limbs. They are itching to get to the show. There is the usual chitchat- how bright the sun is, how great the day is going to be, how hungover they are.

Shrugging on his heavily studded leather jacket, Henry joins them, beat-up soft guitar case in one hand. After the Strat's neck had snapped off at the base, Blower attached a new neck stock and set it up in less than an hour. There wasn't time to refinish the guitar, but Henry prefers it this way- raw, naked, and real. As he starts to settle on the stairs next to Sophie, the van rumbles around the corner and screeches to a stop in front of the house. The punkettes stand back as Max pops the back door open and Henry jumps down the stairs claiming shotgun. Sophie stands and stretches and gives Val a light punch on the shoulder. "See you there." She clambers over Henry to join Max in the back. She's ready to van surf today.

Gabe slaps the side of the van door with his left hand. "Everybody tucked in?!" He shifts and turns in his seat so he can make sure all the doors are shut, the van surfers hanging on. Henry barks, "All accounted for! Let's get!"

2

As the van pulls away, Val stands and joins Bags and the punkettes on the sidewalk. "Might as well move..." They spread out along the sidewalk, loosely stringed together, as they walk the few blocks to Divisadero where they will catch the bus to the Mission. Tee and Steph call out, "Wait"!" as Babs comes running up the street from Pat's house behind them, "Hi!! I'm here too!" She's huffing and puffing just from that short run up the one block. She has dyed and cut her hair so it is now zebra striped red and black in a short wavy mohawk, and she's wearing her signature black bondage pants with multiple straps and chains criss-crossing her legs, buckled tightly above each knee. One of her ragged high tops is flapping at the sole which is quickly falling off with each step. Babs catches up and bends over, placing one hand on each knee. "Whew! I was afraid I missed you! I don't know where we're going exactly, so..." she waves one hand at everyone. "Hi!"

They catch the 7 towards Market and decide en route that it doesn't make sense to head back towards the Mission. They can catch BART at the Civic Center, so they head North and across the Bay to West Oakland. Val is glad Sophie isn't with them. She's in a sweet place in her two-day high right now, and doesn't feel like faking aggression at all the brown and black faces surrounding them as they exit the platform to the street below. The punkettes chat about who they have a 'thing' for, especially that new punk who just hit town. He looks like a red-headed Billy Idol and is full of just the right amount of sexy swagger. Babs makes small comments throughout the trip to no one in particular and everyone around her. She shares her bag of red and black licorice, and picks at speed scabs on the back of her arms. Bags nudges Val every now and then when Babs says something too upside down to ignore. He's also riding that two-day high sweet spot like a secret he and Val are keeping from the others.

They catch the 29 and ride deeper into Berkeley, passing huge warehouses and storage buildings. Val feels like Dorothy of Oz- she is definitely not in San Francisco anymore. They jump the bus at Shellmound and strut up Bay in a loose military formation as they force other pedestrians off the sidewalk. Shoulders back, arms loose in their sockets, they take up space and make heads turn. As they get closer to the park, they begin to see other punks, mohawks, and skins tripping in the same direction. As they reach the south lot, Val notices a couple of beat-up vans with Anarchy signs spray painted on the side doors. Must be in the right place.

Just beyond the parking lot, a temporary fence has been put up, and a few rows of Harley Davidsons flank the parking lot.

There is a wide entrance just to the left of the bikes, where a dozen ragged-looking Hell's Angels stand around, smoking, drinking beer, and letting punks pass through. Bags starts walking faster. They can hear some band playing already, so the show did start on time. He's itching to get into that pit.

Val keeps up with Bags, and the punkettes keep up with Val. Babs bounces from one punkette to another, pointing out everything she thinks they need to see. There are small groups of punks gathered here and there across the mostly sere, grass-less park. A few stunted, parched trees cluster here and there around the perimeter. Otherwise, it's all pale dirt and patchy grass within the boundaries of the park's long, narrow lake on the one side and weed-strewn railroad tracks on the other. Angels stand around here and there, twice as big and dirty as any of the punks they are there to watch over. Halfway across the baked, dusty park, there is a flatbed truck parked parallel to the tracks, top heavy with great black speakers pulsing with the grinding guitar of some band Val doesn't recognize.

At the last minute, a couple of touring bands had backed out, so The Shits were asked to play after all, as well as this other band, whoever they are. She taps Bags on the arm before he can bolt into the mosh pit, which isn't much to look at right now- just a few mohawks throwing their arms around and skip-marching in semi-circles from one side of the stage to the other.

"Who is this?" She asks. Bags squints at the band as though that might help him discover their name. He hasn't heard them before either. "I don't know. Hey!" He calls to a mohawk he recognizes from the Deaf Club and other various shows. "Who is this?" The mohawk says, "Hey Bags. This is uh, some band from Seattle, I think?" He points at the drumkit. The head says The Fartz.

"Ohhhhh... isn't this the band Jello signed? Cool..." Bags punches the mohawk lightly on one arm, taps Val on her arm, and points to the far end of the flatbed, where Sophie is huddled with The Shits, watching the Fartz grind away.

Val works her way around the clumps of punks gathered at the edge of the micro mosh pit to join Sophie and The Shits. The punkettes pause, uninvited, and hitch themselves to a cluster nearby. Babs doesn't know which way to turn or who to follow, so she winds her way past other stragglers to the back of the park, closest to the water and farthest from the grinding noise radiating from the stage. Bags watches from the edge of the pit, daring any of the moshers to clip him and invite him into the dusty arm-swinging action in front of the stage.

Before that happens though, the band winds up their full

eight-minute set. That's all the songs they know. After a few "Fuck you!"s are exchanged between the band and sparse audience, Jello Biafra jumps up on stage to say a few words about The Fartz, welcome everyone again to The Eastern Front show, and introduce the next band, Deadly Reign from Austin, TX. Bags knows this is a sticking point for the guys in The Shits- that so many southern Cali – and what the fuck Texas- bands were on the bill over San Francisco bands. He gets it but doesn't personally care much one way or the other. As long as the music is good and loud and forces you into the pit, he's a happy man.

The day slips by filled with dust devils, Hells Angels, and more punks filing into the park from all sides. The Shits play to a rousing bloody mosh pit- some kid going down and fists striking out until Jello jumps back on stage and shouts at the moshers to calm the fuck down. When The Shits play their last song, Jello vaults himself off the flatbed into the crowd where he is miraculously caught and buoyed into the thick of it, dropped, and moshes to the end of the last note that rings out from Henry's glistening Strat.

The sun is relentless all day. The crowd is covered in sweat and dust, patchouli and sloshed beer. At one point, during either the JFA or Wasted Youth set, someone threw a beer bottle at the band. Then everyone started throwing beer bottles and cans at the band, at each other, at the mosh pit.

Jello got up on stage again and roared at everyone to chill the fuck down. Even the Hells Angels, who seemed more interested in hanging back and hanging onto their own beer bottles, stepped up menacingly. Sure, it was about time for a few heads to roll. The bottle and can throwing stopped. Some folks half-heartedly picked up bottles here and there, everyone looking around sheepishly, that wasn't me man...

As the headliner from the UK, Chron-Gen, started to play, a train whizzed by behind the band, clanking and clacking loud enough to drown out the opening chords to their set. The bass player and drummer switched to a train beat, and the guitarist stood off to the side grinning at the crowd who continued to mosh to the train.

The train slowed down, so the band slowed their train beat too, and the mosh pit also began to thrash more slowly. Val thought it was surreal- like the world was keeping pace with her dissipating high. If she could find a place to shoot up, maybe things would speed up again too. She looked around for a spot. Those bushes over there? Behind the stage? Where was The Shits' van? She couldn't see it anywhere right away, so she nudged Sophie with one shoulder. Both the train and the band were at a volume so she only needed to holler, not scream, into Sophie's ear.

"Where's the van? I need to uh, do something!"

Sophie flattened her lips in a half grimace, half smirk to her friend. "Oh, uh 'something'? You got 'something' for me?" She waits, and Val nods yeah, sure. Sophie points directly behind the flatbed to the van. Val laughs, she swears she looked right there... They walk around the flatbed to the back of the stage, where an Angel holds his hands out to stop them. "Sorry, ladies, backstage only." Sophie stands taller and growls, "No I'm with these guys," and jerks one thumb towards The Shits packing up their gear behind the stage. The Angel says, "Oh right, you came with them." And lets them both pass. Sophie dunks her hand into one of the backstage coolers full of gritty melted ice and grabs one of the last warm bottles of water floating in between a few empty beer bottles and other trash.

As they walk over to the unlocked van, a dust devil magically swirls up around them. Val looks up and notices Max looking over his shoulder at them from behind the flatbed. "Hey!" He calls out. "Where you going?!" Val points in the general direction of the van, which also happens to be the general direction of the train. Max yells again, "Gonna jump the train?!"

Val and Sophie both cackle. "Yeah, right after we lay some tracks first," Sophie snorts. She opens the side door of the van and waits for Val to climb in, then clambering in behind her, pulls the door shut.

The van reeks of motor oil, dust, and sweat. When Val and Sophie remove their sunglasses, they cackle and point. They both have raccoon eyes. Val swipes the back of her arm across her face, smudging the dirt but not dislodging it. She shrugs and digs into her flannel pouch.

The two shoot up, taking care to keep the product and process as clean as possible, even in all this dust. Hell, Sophie's shot up behind reeking dumpsters in the rain, using the dumpster lid as a sort of shelter, greasy funk and all, so a little dirt shouldn't hurt them. Once they've both imbibed, Val licks her spoon clean, then dips her rig into the water bottle, pulls the plunger back, and sprays water against the wall to clear out residue from her works. Sophie pulls her Nuns t-shirt off and throws it onto the small pile of discarded clothing the band has been chucking into the van all day. For a big gal with such broad shoulders, she has small breasts which hang loosely inside the wife beater she wore beneath her t-shirt. It's hot inside the van and smells ripe. With a quick glance to see that Val has packed up shop, Sophie opens the side door, and they both sit in the doorway, stretching their legs, trying to think where to go next.

Chron-Gen has launched into Puppets of War, one of Sophie's new favorite songs, full of driving guitar, cranking drums, and almost tinny vocals riding the music like waves.

Sophie nods her head in time to the song and puts her shades back on. The sun is just starting to edge closer to the horizon, and the heat is less oppressive. But for Val, a full day of sweat and dirt and speed oozing out of her pores has her feeling frowsy and overheated. She looks longingly out towards the water beyond the flatbed and all the arm-swinging, high-stepping moshers. "You think we can jump in the water?"

Sophie thinks about it, scrunching up her nose. "I don't know if I would. There's all those birds and shit. Might not be as refreshing as you think…" Val sighs, yeah, merde… She stands and stretches her arms over her head and sees the train still ambling slowly behind them. "How 'bout we jump the train, like Max said? We can ride up to the next stop. It's got to be cooler with all that air rushing by..?"

Sophie stands and closes the van door. She places her hands in her back pockets and sniffs. Val has never ridden the rails before, so she doesn't know what's what. She turns and leans against the van, flinching at the hot metal on her bare arms. Pushing off from the van, Sophie steps towards the stage. "Let's dunk our heads in the beer cooler."

Val swings her attention to where the Angel is still blocking access to backstage. He's poking some skinny punk with one hand and enjoying it. "That water was pretty hot, actually. Come on, let's jump the train!" She's excited by the idea now. She's heard plenty of stories about other punks' adventures riding the rails. Val thinks it would be a hoot.

Sophie shakes her head no and starts to walk over to the lengthening shadows behind the flatbed. It's got to be cooler there. "I think jumping a train with you would be fun. But you gotta do it prepared. You can't just jump a train. You gotta have water, and food, and warm clothes." She holds her hands up at Val's sputtering protest. "Yeah, I know, it's fucking hot right now. But those trains don't stop at every station. And when they get going, it gets fucking cold, especially at night. So who knows where we'd end up? And we don't have any of the shit we'd need to make it alright." She scratches her neck and inspects the dirt under nails. "You know who knows this shit? Bags. You should ask him about what trains to catch. Like when and where they go, and what to pack and all that."

Val lights up. Right! She forgot that Bags has jumped the train a bunch of times. Didn't he have a story about someone he knows who died? Or got run over and lost a leg or something like that? She reminds herself to talk to him about that. She could maybe bring her paints and draw something new. She looks around for Bags, but he's most definitely in that pit, raging and working the rest of that speed out of his system.

She turns to Sophie and persists, "Well, so what if I get all the stuff we need, and the details from Bags? Do you want to jump the train with me then?" Sophie grunts in reply.

They pause around the left side of the stage in a much cooler wedge of shade. Sophie watches the band. They are playing a song she doesn't know, the guitar pulsing and pulsing, then switching to the band's familiar driving and intense style. Something about lies, huh, she likes it. The mosh pit is going nuts, thrashing and kicking, all arms and legs and angry or smiling faces. Funny how it's all the same in the pit: happy, angry, all the same.

The shit that Val shared with her is really fucking good. She yells, "Let's watch the band! And yeah, let's jump a train!" Val smiles and hangs both thumbs on her belt, now riding low on her hips. Has she lost more weight today? Whatever. She'll go talk to Marco tomorrow and figure out all the health food stuff then.

Val starts rocking back and forth on the heels of her boots and loses herself in the music for the first time today. Too bad it's the last band. The sun has started to set and she's actually starting to shiver a little. She is happy, thinking about this trip she and Sophie will take soon. It will be good to get out of town for a day, give her some new ideas. She scratches her crotch. Shit, time to take a pill, and put some more ointment on. When the band is done, she'll slip into the van and manage that. There's no way she's going into one of those foul bathrooms. They stink and are rank by the end of the day. Earlier, someone tipped one over while some poor Berkeley kid was inside. He must have been about twelve or thirteen, and when he finally got the door open, he stumbled out of the cubicle covered in shit and funk. His shirt and arms were stained blue, and he ran away crying. Poor kiddo. Yeah, no way she's climbing into one of those.

Chron Gen blasts through their powerful set. It's been an amazing show, from local heroes The Shits to The Lewd, Husker Dü, Wasted Youth and so many more bands. Eight hours of crashing, bashing, slamming music. Never mind the Hell's Angels, even though they did rough a few punks up a little. No one was really hurt and no fights broke out. Bags figures, I guess that's good enough reason to have them here. Plus Jello has done an ace job of calming down any punks cruising for a fight.

Bags has stepped out of the mosh pit for another breather. He's been pretty much in and at it most of the day, stepping out for a beer every once in a while, until those ran out. A few times, he stepped aside to let his heart settle and to smear the dust-drenched sweat running down his face and neck. Speed sweat keeps getting in his eyes, so he's been moshing with his eyes squeezed shut, ramming into people and shoulder slamming everyone. He's a little giddy at this point and realizes he's thirsty. He looks around. There nothing left to drink anywhere. He'll get something to drink after the show.

He grins as some kid goes down and has to crawl his way out of the pit. Yeah... live and learn, kid. That's the way the mosh pit crumbles. Bags cracks the knuckles on both hands and twists his head to the left and to the right, with a loud pop in his neck. Looking behind him, he realizes the sun is starting to set. When did that happen? Damn, it's almost dark! So... not much time left to mosh. Might as well get back in there. He watches the melee swing around and around, and breathing in time with the music, Bags throws himself back into the crowd. Suddenly, it's all tats and fists, dust and sweat spattered shoulders, knees and Doc Martens. He recognizes a maniacal grin here, the spike on a wilting mohawk there, slammed by someone's glistening arm and knocked out of sight.

Someone dives off the stage, and is half caught and half dropped to the ground. The punk is spun around with one foot dragging behind him and one leg caught in the twisting, stomping crowd. Grasping hands hold him partly aloft as he struggles to be freed and screams at everyone to let go. Bags reaches in and tries to snatch at one of those hands. His arm is knocked away. He launches himself at the roiling stream of moshers dividing him from the screaming punk and throws a punch at one arm holding the kid up. His fist connects, and the hand connected to that arm drops the punk, who falls, spinning with the pit, to the ground.

The last thing Bags sees of the punk is him rolling up into a ball and being stomped by all the goose-stepping chaos overhead. He briefly thinks he should do something else to help, but is caught up in the round and round, shoulders, fists, knees and boots. He barely hears the music as he swings his arms and moves past the tangle of bodies twisting and untwisting at the center of the pit. Huff and step, swing and step, sweat stinging his eyes, and man this is the life!

Suddenly the music stops. The lead singer yells something into the microphone about this being a blah blah blah something. Bags can't quite understand the fucker's accent. Or maybe it's the spinning in his head that has him unable to hear right. The crowd of punks screams at the band to play one more fucking song. A few call out song titles. But Bags' ears are ringing, and he can't quite understand what anyone is saying. He stands off to the side of the mosh pit even though no one is dancing any more.

He is really thirsty now. While punks around him scream at the band and call them all sorts of names, Bags looks around for Val. He sees a bunch of people he knows, but no-one he wants to talk to right now. He realizes he's crashing and wants to think about making plans to head out, maybe get high again. He still has that last hit left in his wallet. Hopefully it didn't get wet or fucked up somehow in the heat of the day. It's getting dark now, and the only lights in the park are on the flatbed, half blinding Bags, so he looks away.

3

Some bodies start peeling off the clusters of punks here and there, making their way to the rows of Harleys still parked at the entrance to the show. Bags watches them, trying to see if Val is one of them. He doesn't think she would just bail without checking on him first. He decides she must be backstage with Sophie. Would she have left with The Shits? Did they leave? He doesn't remember any vehicles driving away from behind the stage. But he doesn't remember the sun setting, or what anyone not in the pit has been doing. He makes his way over to the side of the stage, looking for Val's flannel and week old stubble and fringe. The stage lights keep blinding him. He's not sure if maybe he's passed her already, so he swings around and tries to peer into the darkness around him. He's coming down harder now and really needs a drink.

"Bags!" Val's voice trills into his ear. Relieved, he spins around. She is backlit by a halo of light leaving her face darkened and bleary to his speed-addled eyes. "There you are! Where have you been all day?"

Bags shuffles to her side so he can see her face. He shades his eyes with one hand, even as he peers into the dark. "I've been slamming all day. Mosh pit. Fucking great day."

Val grins happily. "Bah, I kept meaning to mosh, but it was too intense all day, and I'm still feeling all itchy down below, not so great." She waves one hand in a vague circle around her crotch. "So I hung out with Sophie backstage most of the day." She checks out Bags' eyes, spinning and unfocused. "Oooooh, someone is finis for the day!" Bags sways a little on his feet. "Damn, yeah. I was just thinking I need a drink and my last hit."

Feedback suddenly strikes the air around them, causing Val to jump. Up on the flatbed, Chron Gen leans into their instruments and thrashes out one last song for the taunting crowd, 'Jet Boy Jet Girl'. Most of the punks streaming out of the park stop, turn around, and come running or walk quickly back towards the stage. The mosh pit immediately starts churning right next to where Val and Bags are standing. A boot kicks out and clips Val in the back of one leg. She flinches, and he shoots an arm out to protect her from the flailing bodies trying to suck them into the vortex of the pit. He pulls her further away from the stage and pit and stands there with his arm around her shoulders. She grins up at him.

"If you want to get back in there, go!" Bags looks over at the mass of dancers gleefully slamming into one another. His brain is as fried as his vision though- too much sun, coming down hard now, and besides... Val is grinning at him like...? He scrunches up his face and shakes his head, nah... "I'm flat-lined. I need a drink of water or something. Maybe find someplace to hit before heading back. After this." He gestures to the stage and nods his head in time to the out-of-control cadence of the song, making sure to keep his arm slung over Val's shoulder. She doesn't say anything, so he closes his eyes and enjoys the feeling of the earth slipping from beneath his feet. Somehow, he is still standing. His brain is lightly rattling in its cage, in time to the beat of the song. Bags likes Chron Gen's version so much better than the Damned's slower more melodic recording. If they keep playing, maybe he won't crash so hard.

Val stands there grinning so hard her cheeks hurt. Bags' arm feels perfect right where it is. She keeps having to remind herself to breathe; she doesn't want to change anything and spoil the moment. She is cresting her second high of the day and feels so good. The music crashes like waves inside her head. Rush rush rush go the drums. Rwowr rwowr wah goes the guitar. 'Jet Boy Jet Girl Gonna take you round the world' the lyrics stream like a ticker tape across her mind's eye. Wooooosh her heart is pounding, and she feels light on her feet, like she might float away on the music, the chaos of the moshers off to the side, Bag's touch on her bare shoulders. A shiver runs through her body. Val looks at Bags to see if he's noticed., but his eyes are still clenched shut. He's still nodding hard in time to the song.

Chron Gen plays the final triple hit hard, and the song rings out in a rippling echo as the crowd hollers and spits at the stage. That was exactly the best way to end the show! The moshers stand around looking at each other and the band, who have retreated to the back of the flatbed. Jello doesn't even take the stage again. Some other punk steps up and yells a bunch of unintelligible words into the microphone, something about pick up your trash, be cool with the neighborhoods as you leave, blah blah blah. Val looks at Bags again and sees him looking right back at her. So...

"I'm really high right now. Sophie and I just set up in the van. Maybe you can...?" she offers. She doesn't want his arm to go anywhere, but maybe she can keep this, whatever this is between them, going. Bags peers into the dark area behind the still-brightly lit stage. He thinks he sees The Shits' van but can't tell for sure. "You know where the van is? I could use something right about now."

Val wraps the arm closest to Bags around him and, hand lightly on his hip, nudges him towards the backstage area. Is it possible that her high just ratcheted up a notch? Eeeee Bags... The backstage Angel is nowhere to be seen and someone has overturned the trash-filled cooler. Val hopes

Sophie left that water bottle in the van. She hopes The Shits don't mind if they use the van for a few minutes. She hopes the van is still there. She steers Bags in the direction of where she thinks the van is and sees Sophie suddenly from the corner of her high, her eye, heh heh. Oh yeah, she is flying now.

"Hey Sophie!" Val waves with her free hand. "Did The Shits leave?"

Sophie smiles at Val and Bags with a wicked glint in her eye. "I knew it! I knew this would happen! It's about time!" She cocks one thumb over her shoulder, "Yeah, the van is right there," - a little to the right of where Val had remembered it. Bags smiles sheepishly. Yeah, he knew it too. He just didn't know how or when. Evidently, now and here. Val says, "No no!! It's not for... this. Is the water bottle still in the van? Bags needs to use the facilities for a minute. If the guys don't mind?"

Sophie looks over her shoulder, "Nah, if you're quick, they can pile everything up outside the van. They're still talking to all their adoring fans." She points at the flatbed, where The Shits, Chron Gen, and a few other straggler bands who haven't left yet are surrounded by punkettes and punks, starstruck and reaching out to touch their constellations.

She walks Val and Bags over to the van, just to be sure it's ok. But none of the band is there, so she opens the van door, urges the two inside, and stands guard leaning against the closed door while they fix Bags up.

Inside the van, Val waits for her eyes to adjust to the dark. There is no overhead light; the bulb has been broken for longer than anyone can remember. She feels around for the water bottle, and voila! Success. Bags sits next to one of the overturned crates and pokes around his wallet until he touches the cellophane baggie. Feels dry, though kinda warm to the touch. Should be ok. "Isn't there a light in here somewhere?" he asks.

Val bangs on the door, and Sophie peeks inside. "Is there a flashlight? It's fucking dark in here." Sophie thinks a moment, and says "Yeah, in that thing hanging over the driver's seat." And points to the beaded seat cover with a flap hanging over the back. Bags reaches inside and pulls out a hefty flashlight. Of course, Sarge would insist on this kind of tool, he thinks. "Thanks Sophie, do you mind...?" "Oh yeah," she shuts the door again and stands guard.

While Bags holds the flashlight and tries to unspool the little baggie between the fingers of his other hand, Val remembers he needs to use her works, so she roots around in her pouch, finds what he needs, and scootches closer to him to set everything up on the overturned crate. Spoon, water, rig. She pinches a small piece of cotton and rolls it between her fingers, waiting for Bags to take the next step. "Do you want me to hold that?" she asks.

"Yeah, I was trying to figure out how I was gonna do this." He smiles at her. "Thanks." He hands her the flashlight, which she holds aloft over the laid-out set up. Bags empties the last of his speed into the spoon, careful not to spill any. He picks up the rig, lowers it into the water bottle, pulls back on the plunger, and sprays a small amount against one wall.

Needle back into the bottle, pull back plunger, carefully dribble water into and around the speed in the spoon. He stirs the speed gently with the tip of the needle and Val drops the cotton ball into the mix. Bags places the edge of the needle tip against the cotton- not in the cotton, no way- he's had cotton fever before and doesn't need to experience that ever again, thank you very much. Concentrating, he pulls back on the plunger to drink up all the liquified meth, upends the needle and taps any air bubbles up and out, and depresses the plunger ever so slightly. Then needle between teeth, Val's proffered belt around upper arm, tight, tighter. Pump fist one two three times until a good vein pops up. He's always had good veins. He's lucky that way.

He trades the end of the belt for the needle between his teeth, angles the needle just so against his raised vein, and inserts it gently, quickly, smack dab in the middle of the vein. Pull back on the plunger to release a cloud of billowing beautiful blood. Press down on the plunger slowly, steadily, release the belt. He puts the works down, Removes the belt from his arm, and coughs with a little explosion of chemical heat at the back of his throat. He whistles between the gap in his front teeth. "Pheeeew! Yeah! Fuck yeah!"

Val cleans the needle while Bags crests this first part of the high. Once he focuses on her, his lips pulled back into a twisted smile against dry teeth, she picks up the spoon. "Do you mind if I...?" The spit has dried up in his mouth. There's no way he could take the metallic crunch of the cotton ball right now. "Oh yeah, it's all yours." She pops the cotton ball in her mouth, licks the spoon, wipes it on her flannel, and packs everything away while she sucks the dregs of meth from the tiny bit of cotton. She trembles. Brrr... one of those metallic, chemical shivers that start at your teeth and work their way down to your toes.

Once everything is put away, Val hands the flashlight back to Bags. They look at each other, yeah? Yeah. Bags opens the door and steps out as Sophie steps away from the van. "Not that I was listening or anything, but man, you two are quiet..." she gives that same wicked grin again.

Val flushes and looks at Bags. Bags looks at Val. "Ha. Not yet, Sophie. You'll know if you hear it." He throws his arm around Val's shoulder again and pulls her in. Val squeals. He smells like speed and sweat, sun and dirt. And something else. A Bags smell, though she can't quite put her finger on what that is. Kind of like a caramel apple? Whatever it is, she likes it. Her skin is tingling where he's touching her. In fact, her whole body is tingling. Sure, that's the speed, but Bags is like the meth cherry on top. She leans in and licks his arm. Salty, musky, and there– sweet like– not quite like a caramel apple, but something. Never mind. Bags looks pleasantly surprised, "What the...?"

Henry marches over to the van, guitar case in one hand, Orange speaker cab in the other. He moves towards the back of the van. "Hey! A little help?" Sophie trots around the back of the van, pops the door open, and Henry drops his gear inside. "Do you mind...?" he asks Sophie. She knows the drill. Never leave the gear unattended. She slaps him on the ass. "Go. I got this."

Val and Bags are just standing there, feeling his arm on her shoulders. Feeling the high between them, and this other thing over the top of that too. "Hey Sophie..." Val says. "We're gonna head back to the City now. See you at Pat's?"

"Yeah. We're gonna pick up some beer, see you there."

Bags brushes his fingers against Val's shoulder and urges her away from the van. He looks up and notices the train still parked on the tracks. "Huh, too bad I don't have my kit with me. We could jump that train."

Val looks at Sophie who starts cackling. "I told you so!!"

The other two Shits stumble up to the van with heavy armloads of drums, stands, and bass cabinet. Sophie steps back to give them room to arrange things just so- van Tetris- as Bags and Val say bye to everyone and make their way towards the rows of Harleys now dwindling at the entrance to the park.

"So I'm supposed to ask you about that, jumping a train..."

"A city is where you can sign a petition, boo the chief justice, fish off a pier, gape at a hippopotamus, buy a flower at the corner, or get a good hamburger or a bad girl at 4 a.m. A city is where sirens make white streaks of sound in the sky and foghorns speak dark grays — San Francisco is such a city." — **Herb Caen**

Sisterhood of Night-Light

1

The streetlights are bright haloes, reverberating off the wet tarmac and buildings below. A siren screams in the distance, first moving in, then farther away. Bab's footsteps echo on the wet pavement. She wishes she still had her skateboard. But Annie X had taken that as rent in kind for the little room she sometimes sleeps in at the back of Annie's Haight squat. Babs wishes she had her rat for company. But the rat disappeared into the bowels of the squat over a week ago and hasn't been seen since. Every now and then, as she burns candles and tries her hand at casting spells in the narrow maid's room she can't think of as her own, Babs hears tiny scrunching noises from behind the walls. She's sure it's her rat, and calls out 'Luna...!' softly, not wanting to disturb whatever Annie is doing in the other room. But Luna hasn't shown up for her treats and scratches, so maybe it's some other rat. Maybe Luna is dead. Babs can't think about that now.

Now, she is on a mission to find speed. Annie hasn't been home in a few days, and Babs has no idea where she might be or when she might return. They don't tell each other that sort of thing. Annie is there or she's not, and then she's there again. Babs thinks they should have one of those doctor's 'In/Out' boards, but Annie would knock that idea down like she does Babs' other suggestions for the apartment. Annie makes damned clear it's not Babs' apartment in any way. Even though it's a squat, it belongs to Annie X, so what she says, goes.

Babs had suggested they turn the kitchen into an artist lab of sorts. Get rid of the fridge and stove, since they're never used, and add a workbench and barstools. Rent the space out to punks who don't have anywhere else to do whatever it is they might want to do: paint, photography, leather tooling and cutting, sewing like Kelly-Belly from that squat on Fell does. She also suggested they collect dead animals- cats and rats and birds- and dry the bodies out so they can strip everything from the bones, then sell the skeletons to punks who are into that sort of thing. Every idea she has brought up has been shot down. Too bad, Babs thinks- she gets great ideas when she's high and would love to make at least one of them come true- also while high, of course. That's when she gets her best work done. Just last month, she helped Steve with his schoolwork over at UCSF by typing up all his papers for him. He'd gotten her high, and she typed like a banshee. She thought she'd done an excellent job. Steve got so mad at her though because she didn't know you shouldn't capitalize all the words you thought were important, only names of places and people and things like that, it turns out.

Before he kicked her out of his place, she thought she would advertise over at the college and type papers for other students too. Since Steve said he didn't want to see her for a while, and it was his typewriter, she gave up on that idea. The other idea that she and Amy over at Pat's house had come up with late one night was that of a house cleaning company called Dirty Deeds Done Dirt Cheap. They'd figured out what they needed to buy and where they would store everything and how they would split up the duties. They even sketched out flyers, thinking they would ask Amy's Clits pal Val to create more eye-catching flyers they could copy off and distribute all over the Haight. Babs was very excited about that plan, but then Amy skipped town. Maybe Babs can find someone else to run that project with her?

She pauses at the corner of Page and Central to re-fasten the gauze she has wrapped around her legs as stockings. They keep unravelling so she has to stop and adjust them every block or so. Sometimes Babs buys enough meth to get high, sell tenths, and earn enough to buy more. Sometimes, folks trade items with her for the speed she is selling. That's how she acquired a spool of loose, wide medical gauze that she immediately cut up and started wearing. She dons a pair of faded black culottes she's had forever, then pinning one end of a long strip of gauze behind each knee, she tightly winds each strip around her legs until they end at her ankles, where she tucks them into her high-tops. The safety pin keeps tearing through the unraveling gauze at one knee, so Babs unwraps and rewinds the gauze tighter, safety pins it in place and stands to admire her handiwork.

Babs knows plenty of other punkettes from the Vats who are also wearing this gauze, though differently than she does. They tug open strips on as leggings or over their arms as diaphanous sleeves. Babs desperately wants to be different than everyone else though, so she wears her gauze this way instead. She feels like a punk time traveler from the 1920's. Like a doughboy? Or is that earlier? Or later? Anyway, that's what she thinks.

As Babs skips across the street, happy happy happy to be on her mission, and happy happy happy there are no people on the street somehow at this hour- it's only three am- where is everyone? She tries to remember the name of the punkette who told her where to go. Suzie? Stinie? Steph?

She thinks it's Steph, who told Babs to meet her at 712 Ashbury, sometime after three. Steph said she was picking up some meth and would introduce Babs to the seller too. That's a big deal, since most of the sellers Babs buys from never want her to meet their sources. It's all very tied down, hush-hush and secretive that way. She thinks maybe she can buy extra, do less, sell more, and keep doing that until she is a bigger dealer like Shelly or Annie. She could move out of Annie's tiny back room, get her own place, and do whatever the hell she wants there. Her heart beats faster just thinking about it.

Babs turns on Waller up towards Haight. These houses are all so pretty, she thinks. It would be fun to paint one all black with silver streaks and polka dots. Maybe that's what she'll do when she's a bigger dealer. She thinks about the furniture she will fill the house with– a Rocky Horror lips couch and Clockwork Orange tables. She will wallpaper the place with show posters and drawings cut out of children's picture books. And that artist lab, for sure. And... she stops. What is the address again? She pivots on one foot, trying to see if there is something that can remind her. She just had it...

On the steps of a grey, slightly decrepit big old house, a hippie is sitting cross-legged. He's wrapped up in a fuzzy rainbow poncho of some kind and has one fat blond dreadlock sticking out from the side of his head. His face is covered with a darker blond scratchy looking beard– Babs hates beards– and his eyes are closed.

"Hey!" Babs skips over to stand in front of the grey house. "Do you know where Ed the light guy lives?" No answer. "HEY!"

The hippie opens one eye, sighs, and turns both hands from where they'd been face up on each leg to face down, cupping each knee. "I'm meditating, man. This is a holy spot." Babs snorts. "Oh, ok, do you know where Ed the light guy lives? I'm supposed to meet a friend there."

The hippie raises both hands to gesture at the house behind him. "I don't know, man. I just know here. I don't know Ed."

Babs takes a deep breath, and placing her hands on her hips, leans to the left to see if that house might be it, then to the right to see if maybe that house will point her way. Suddenly she notices, in one house further to the right, a light burning brightly in the front room. She trips up the street to stand in front of this purple Jimi Hendrix place– who would paint a house this crazy color? she wonders. She has completely forgotten about the hippie, and is now standing tiptoe, trying to see behind the mostly pulled down shades. As she's teetering and distracted by that, a face peers out at her from beneath one of the shades. It's Steph! Steph beckons to Babs and points to the front door. Babs gives her the thumbs up with both hands and skips up the stairs. Her heart is pounding again. Sheesh, she used to be able to skate all day and run and climb trees. Now, just climbing a small flight of stairs and her heart is leaping up into her throat. She needs to only do better drugs from now on, she thinks.

She reaches the top of the stairs and the front door opens a crack. Some old hippie guy with a bandana around his head and a long, thin grey ponytail peers at her from behind the chain on the door. Babs giggles. "Hi, is Steph here?" The hippie guy asks, "You Babs? You alone?" Babs nods, yes and yes. "Steph told me to meet her here. Are you... Ed?" She hopes she remembers that right. The hippie guy closes the door slightly, removes the chain, and opens the door wide enough for Babs to squeeze through. "In, in. Get in here." She steps through.

Steph is in a brightly lit anteroom just beyond the split hall/stairwell entryway. She waves at Babs. "Ed, that's her. Babs, come back here." Ed steps back and gestures for Babs to go ahead of him. He locks the door behind her and follows. Babs smiles nervously at Steph. It's only the three of them there. She doesn't know this hippie guy Ed and she doesn't know how to act. "Hi, sorry I'm a little late. I got a little turned around, the streets are so empty..."

Steph says "Phh, you're not late. Right on time." She beams. "So, Ed, Babs. Babs, Ed." There is a scarred round table in the middle of the anteroom covered with papers and old books. Ed passes behind Babs to stand in a doorway to one side of the table. Legal boxes and produce cartons are stacked against the walls all around the room, some towering nearly as tall as Ed. Across the space is a large square entrance to the front room with the blinds that Steph had peered through. More boxes are stacked against the doorjamb, partly blocking access to the larger room.

Babs sees a jumble of furniture and large metal copiers or photography gear of some kind? She remembers Steph telling her something about this guy doing some kind of light show. Weren't they supposed to do something at the Eastern Front show the other week? Babs had gone with a group of punks she knew from around town, including Steph and her pals, but had quickly lost track of everyone at the show and never caught up with them again. She became de-hydrated and dizzy and began to feel ill, so she left the show early, after only two or three bands. If there had been a light show, she missed it. She realizes no-one has said anything for a while. "Uh hey, is that the light show stuff you were telling me about?" She asks Steph.

Ed tilts his chin up at the other room, "Yeah, that's my gig. Brotherhood of Light. You ever seen us?"

Babs has to say no, though now she wishes she could say yes so they have something to talk about "I think... you did something at the Eastern Front last weekend? I got sick and had to leave early. I missed it. Steph was helping you, wasn't she?"

Steph leans back against some of the boxes and crosses her arms. "Yeah, Ed is teaching me about mixing the oils and how to run things. It's fun. The show was killer. You should have seen all the punks moshing in the lights." She looks at Ed. "There's more shows coming up. Something for some Grateful Dead anniversary thing, and some free concert in the park. I'll let you know."

Babs thinks to herself, remember the name: Brotherhood of Night, right? She has no fucking clue what she would do at a Grateful Dead show. Cool name though, makes her think of vampires, which she likes.

Ed nods. "So Steph says you're looking for some meth in quantity. Whatchya got in mind? Here, let's move back here." He gestures at the doorway he is standing in. Babs steps towards Ed, then changes her mind and goes the long way around the table, to follow Steph into the room. She heard what happened to Shelly and is nervous around men she doesn't know from the scene. Ed chuckles. "It's alright. Grab a chair. Let's talk business."

Ed's chuckling makes Babs think maybe he is a nice man, like an uncle or something. She relaxes a little as they walk into a small room just off the kitchen. The ceiling is partly sloped by the staircase that runs overhead. There is another round table in the middle of this room, but no papers or books. The table has a large sheet of heavy plastic draped over the top, with a fresh pad of legal lined paper, a single pen, and a small black gun, laid out side by side. Babs startles at the sight of the gun, but she tries to play it cool. She reaches out to touch the stiff plastic sheet where it hangs over the edges of the table in stiff waves. Hm, a dress would be cool made out of this stuff...

Steph sits and Babs does too, just to the left and right of the doorway through which they have come. Ed sits in front of the legal pad-pen-gun display. He clears his throat. "So, quantity? What are you looking for?" Babs looks at Steph, then back at Ed. She can't buy any quantity. What did Steph tell him? What did she tell Steph? She thinks quickly, but nothing comes to mind.

"Um, I only need to buy a quarter ounce now." Then it comes, "I was thinking try that out, see how it goes. And then come back for more quantity." She uses the word he's using, hoping he buys it. She doesn't know how she could pull this off, unless she can sell something or borrow money from someone. She's pretty sure this Ed guy won't front her the speed, even if Steph did introduce them.

Ed leans back in his chair. "Huh, ok. That's good thinking. You don't know me. I don't know you. Let's do this, and if you like what I have to offer, move up to a higher level." Babs snorts, he said 'higher'. Steph knows why Babs has snorted, and smiles, "Yeah, higher, heh." Babs blushes a little. She doesn't want to seem like a novice. She's cool! She is an experienced dealer! Just never at a 'higher' level. She knows this is where she belongs though. She just has to follow her plan: sell more, do less, buy more, repeat. Then she can have all the things she keeps tweaking on and make them real, not just speed-induced fantasies. She can do this.

Steph is cleaning her nails with a toothpick she pulled from somewhere. Babs wishes she had a toothpick too. She realizes Ed is waiting for her to say something. "Yup, that's what I'm thinking. I have the money...?" Ed waves her off. "No, let's test the product first. Make sure this is something you want to get into. I don't buy from another supplier. My guy runs his own lab. So what you taste here is what you get every time. You get consistency and your clients will appreciate knowing what they're going to get from you every time."

Babs loses her breath for a second. Her brain starts bouncing with ideas, oh my God, he's right! This is a big deal! She's never been anywhere even remotely close to this kind of set up. She has to, absolutely has to make this work. First this quarter, then an ounce, then two, then four... then a half pound! And then... She can be a big-time dealer, bigger than Annie X, as big as Shelly, but without the scary kidnapper boyfriend.

Ed stands. "Ok, I'll be right back." Babs looks at Steph with wide eyes. She whispers, "Oh my God Steph! I didn't know! This guy's kind of a big deal!" Steph leans over the table, arms tucked by her sides. "Didn't I tell you? He's got some kind of connection with the Hell's Angels. All I know is his shit is great, and he has no one lined up to distribute for him outside of all those bikers. He doesn't want to sell to anyone who's carrying other product, and he wants to break into the punk scene. I thought you would be great, since you go to so many shows and seem to be everywhere."

Babs looks nervously at the gun. "What about that?" Steph laughs, "Oh you think that's scary? Look at this." She reaches behind her and shifts a long roll of paper that is leaning against the corner behind her chair to reveal a long black and shiny shotgun of some kind. Babs doesn't know a thing about guns, but she does know, from TV and movies, that that is a shotgun. And some other shorter and narrower long-barreled guns nestled in behind it. Babs squirms in her chair. "What...?! I can't, I don't..." she doesn't know what to think or say or do. She's in this now. "Why does he have all these guns?" she whispers. Steph moves the paper roll back into place. "He's..."

"He's got friends who aren't exactly friends if you know what I mean. This is a serious business, and sometimes serious people don't take me too seriously. So I have to stand up and make sure they do." Ed comes back into the room carrying a small frameless oval mirror with lines laid out on it already. He sets the mirror down in front of Babs. "Don't worry about the guns. You don't have to see them if you don't like them. We'll do drops someplace where there aren't any, cool?"

Babs smiles nervously, trying not to show her fear. Smile bigger. No, smile less big. "Cool," she croaks. She clears her throat. "Yeah, I'm not... I don't know anything about guns. They kinda scare me a little? So that would be good."

Ed hands Babs a nice, crisp rolled-up bill. "Well, first

thing's first. Let's see what's what, and if you like what we got going on here, we can talk about all that other stuff down the road."

Babs takes the rolled-up bill, inserts it into one nostril, and placing her free hand over the hanging jangle of chains and crosses at her neck, bends over the mirror. She presses the pinky of her rolled-up bill holding hand to her free nostril, then snorts half of one long line. She removes the straw from her nostril, sniffs back any residue and immediately feels an exquisite tingling sensation in the crease of her elbows, behind her eyeballs, and the tips of her toes. She switches the rolled-up bill to her other nostril, pinky-pinches her free nostril shut, and snorts up the rest of that line. She almost licks the rolled-up bill, but then realizes no-one else has used it yet, and offers it to Ed, who gestures to Steph. "Steph, go ahead. Same as last batch."

Steph takes the bill from Babs, slides the mirror her way, and snorts up the other long line in two parts. "Ahhhhhhhh!!" she half croaks half sighs. Steph shivers like a dog shaking off water. "That. Is. The. Shit."

Babs is grinning hard now. The creases of her smile hurt. Her eyes feel like they are spring loaded and about to shoot out at whatever she looks at too closely. She closes her eyes briefly, to calm them down, and swallows the drip coming down the back of her throat. Yeah, this is the shit. It tastes clean and bright. She can tell the high will be clean and bright too- it already is.

Ed leans back in his chair. "Ok, so take a quarter now. If your clients like it, come back for what? Quarter pound? Is that a good starting point?" Babs' grin falters. "Or... 2 ounces? What you got in mind?"

Babs thinks about what she can sell, or who might be able to lend her that money without wanting in on the deal, or even needing to know why, really. She sees various punks' faces she knows in her mind- not him, not her, she doesn't have any money, he'll want a piece of this... Then it strikes her- Carla! Carla has money! And Carla isn't interested in dealing! Carla likes Babs, or at least she thinks she does. Yes, yes. Carla will want to buy from her too, a lot, Babs thinks. She smiles.

"Yup, I just want to run this past a couple of people who are regulars of mine," she exaggerates, wanting to seem like she's a bigger dealer than she is. "Then I think a quarter pound should be a good place to start. I should be able to do that tomorrow. Uh, later today?" She grins. Yeah this shit is GOOD.

Steph is going at her nails with that toothpick now, digging out more debris between skin and nail even though they're clean. Ed taps both hands flat on the table. "That's a plan!" He thinks a moment. "I have an appointment at ten tonight, so we can't meet up then for about an hour. And I'm with my old lady all day, so that's no good. I know we said we would do drops elsewhere, but I don't have anything in mind. So if it's going to be later tonight, then how about eleven? Twelve?"

Babs ponders a moment. Fuck, she really wishes she still had her skateboard. "Um, sure, let's meet at eleven." She should be able to get to Carla's, convince her to lend Babs the money, and get back here by then.

Ed clears his throat and reaches into the pocket of his soft blue Chambray shirt. He hands Babs a business card with a full color image of a taxi on one side and a name and number hand-written on the back. "Call and ask for Buddy. He works nights. He does me favors. He'll give you a ride for a taste."

Babs takes the card and places it on the table in front of her. She's hoping for another line, so she looks at Steph to buy time.

Ed taps the table again with both hands. "Ok, so you still want just the one quarter now?" Babs nods yes. If he doesn't offer any more freebies, she can take a little off the top. Or get Carla to share some with her. Or both. Yeah, both. Ed stands and leaves the room again. Babs reaches across the table, runs a finger through the residue dusting the mirror, and polishes her upper teeth and gums with it. Ooooo tastes good, not like the harsh chemical tang she normally drags across her gums. Steph does the same to 'her' line, and places the toothpick between her teeth, flicking it up and down. "So…?" she raises her eyebrows and flicks the toothpick up.

Babs taps her fingers on the plastic tablecloth. "Shit yeah. This is good." She looks around, "What time is it?" Steph glances into the kitchen. There must be a clock in there that Babs can't see. "It's almost four." Steph bops herself on the forehead with the palm of one hand. "I was going to try to get some sleep tonight, but I guess that's not happening." Babs doesn't pay attention to anything Steph says after 'almost four'. She's trying to think if Carla might still be up. Or if she should wait until later. But what if Carla is up now and then sleeping later? She should make her way over to North Beach, and if Carla isn't up, she can hang at one of the Italian coffee shops and do something– crosswords, or plan out her budget, or write letters– and keep checking in until she catches Carla at some point. Then the speed will do its own selling, and Babs just needs to ask for a small loan. Oh shit. She didn't ask how much!

2

Ed comes back into the room and places a quarter gram of speed, nicely folded in its clean paper envelope, on the table. "Usually that would be eighty bucks. Seventy-five to you. The more you buy, of course, the more the price drops."

Babs looks up at the ceiling and does a quick calculation. She only has seventy dollars. She was planning to buy some beer once the corner stores open up. Shit. "Um hey Ed, sorry. I only have sixty-five bucks. Can I... owe you?" She grimaces lightly, expecting a resounding no. He nods. "Smart. You don't carry a lot of cash on you. This one time, since this is your taster, that's ok." Babs breathes out and starts to push her chair back. He holds a hand up. "Wait, wait. One more thing." Babs leans forward, eager to get this over with and get to Carla's.

"I know you said you're uncomfortable with guns. But I think we should talk about that. Tonight, when you come back, let's talk about what kind of weapon you should carry."

Babs turns her head to one side and looks up at Ed through her lashes. "What...? I don't, uh, know anything about guns. You really think I should carry a gun?"

Ed places the fingertips of both hands on the table. "Yup. And it's ok that you don't know much about them. I can teach you. I have a ranch up north we can go do target practice at. Steph can come if you want. But if you're going to be moving the amount of meth I think we're going to move, you need some protection." He holds up one hand. "Even if it's just preventative. Something to show anyone who might not take you seriously that you are."

Oh... Babs gets it. Yes, she is serious. Yes, she will get a gun, she guesses. "Oh, ok. I don't... I don't even know what I would get?"

Ed smiles faintly. "We'll talk about it tonight. I've got a few options I have in mind for you. Something like a Colt .38 snub nosed revolver. I think that should be just about right. You're small and that should fit comfortably in your hand. You can conceal it easily. We'll need to go over gun safety, on top of target practice. We don't want you doing something stupid and discharging it in public. Safety never takes a day off."

Babs imagines herself holding a gun. How would she carry it? Where would she hide it? Where would she keep it at Annie's so that Annie doesn't find it? She knows Annie goes through her room and things all the time. "Ok..." she says absently. She's been fingering the wad of bills folded in her pocket. She should have peeled off a five while Ed was out of the room. She forgets she didn't know the price before he came back in. She pulls the money out of her pocket and unfolds it. She thumbs through it just to be sure. Yup seventy dollars. "Hey, I do have seventy bucks." She hands him the bills. "Here ya go."

Ed takes the money and hands a five-dollar bill back to Babs. "We said sixty-five. So that's good."

"Oh!" Babs remembers. "How much for the quarter pound? When I come back?" Ed smiles and shakes his head. "Right, did we not go over that? For you, one thousand bucks an ounce. Thirty-seven fifty a quarter pound. Street value, you can get seven thousand to eighty-four hundred for the ounce, more-or-less, depending on how you sell it off." He pauses. "Of course, you know all that."

Babs nods, yup, she knows all that. "Yup, that's a great price, thanks." Now how to ask Carla for three thousand, seven hundred and fifty dollars... she looks at Ed, looks at Steph. "Are we done for now?" Ed folds the bills up and places them in his shirt pocket. "Yup. Good doing business with you. I'll see you later tonight. And don't forget..." he points to the little envelope laying on the table. "Right!" Babs scoops up the envelope and places it carefully at the bottom of her knickers pocket. "Steph, you coming?"

Ed gestures towards the door leading to the front hall. "I'm done for the night. Steph, see you in a couple of days. We'll go over mixing techniques, alright?" Steph mumbles 'yeah, cool' and trips down the hallway. He nods at Babs, "And I'll see you later tonight. Quarter pound, thirty-seven fifty. Try not to get here early. The appointment I have at ten isn't happy about meeting other folks."

"Got it. Thanks for the taxi guy too. See you tonight." Ed follows Babs to the door, opens it for the two girls, and ushers them outside. "Goodnight, ladies." He shuts the door, and a few moments later, the front room light shuts off. Babs wonders if she'll get to sit in that room next time. She turns to Steph. "Ok! What now? Where you going?" She skips down the stairs, loving the way the cool pre-dawn air feels on her face and arms. She doesn't wait for an answer. "I'm heading over to North Beach, to... North Beach." She realizes she shouldn't say Carla's name, to keep her a secret.

Steph takes the steps one at a time, softly stomping in her heavy military-style boots. They're not real military boots, but copies, some Eastern European knockoffs. They almost fit. She has toilet paper crammed up in the toes, but they're still loose, so she tromps around to keep from tripping over her own feet. She yawns and her jaw cracks. "I'm gonna head home." As they reach the bottom of the stairs,

Babs realizes she has no idea where Steph lives. She starts to turn right at the street, as Steph turns to their left. "Oh, ok, goodnight! And thank you so much Steph! I'll owe you big time..."

As Babs turns away from Steph, her mind starts racing with numbers and ideas- thirty-seven hundred fifty dollars. Thirty-two hundred dollars. Buy more, do less, sell more, repeat. Get a place she can paint black and silver. Get some cool furniture and a real mattress. Get a new tattoo. A bat! She can call her place the Bat Cave! No posters and children's book artwork on the walls- pictures of bats! And bat skeletons! Oh she can hardly wait.

She drifts down Waller and up Central, where she'll make her way eventually to the lower Haight. She figures she can catch a bus there. What time do they run? Up towards the big tower on Telegraph Hill. Maybe Carla will be awake. Maybe that café she likes will be open if she has to wait. Babs daydreams as she walks. The houses she passes are sparkling and shimmering, small shafts of mysterious light shoot from odd corners here and there. She can't see where the light is coming from and she doesn't have the time to stop and find out.

On lower Haight, she catches a bus that runs up Market to Union Square. The city is just starting to wake up. Babs is pretty sure those were angels singing in the trees before she got on the bus. City angels, she's certain of it. They sounded like birds, but they were Angels. They hid just out of sight every time she turned to see them.

The sky is turning a soft, dark grey- crackling and fizzing like snow on the TV when programming is over for the night. On the 45 through Chinatown, Babs leans her head against the bus window and watches the buildings streak by. Green and orange tiled roofs bookended by figures of dragons, cryptic Chinese writing, a pagoda roof. The neighborhood changes as they enter North Beach with its cafes and colorfully painted storefronts. Babs gets off the bus just past Vallejo and walks up past Café Greco to Carla's place. She hopes Carla is up. She hopes Carla is home. She can hardly wait to tell Carla about the Brotherhood of Night and her plans for the Bat Cave.

She scans the sidewalk and gutter for treasure. Shiny things catch her eye, but nothing makes her stop. Once, she found a hundred-dollar bill in the gutter. Another time, a small baggie of speed. She's pretty sure it was speed. It was slightly damp, and right after she snorted it, she needed to shit. But it made her go up up and away, and she'd found it, so whatever it was didn't matter at all. Babs' eyes flit this way and that, but there is no treasure today. She realizes as she starts to cross the street that she already passed Carla's place, so she spins on her toes and walks back the way she came, this time looking up at the second floor, not at the street and potential for shiny things there.

Three doors back, she stands beneath Carla's tiny balcony, the one with the heavy chain and lock wound around the rail. That's how Babs knows she in the right spot. If Carla ever removed that chain and lock, Babs might not recognize Carla's place. She can never remember the address. She calls up, softly at first, "Carla! Hey, Carla! You home?" A soft early dawn breeze flutters past Babs, whispering secrets she could know if she listened hard enough. But no distractions. She needs Carla. Again, a little louder now, "Carla!" Babs can't purse her lips but she tries to whistle anyway. It comes out of her mouth in a soft rustle of air. She calls out, "Woooo! Carla! Awoooo!" like a wolf.

Carla's white-blonde cap of spiky hair pokes out over the top of the balcony. It worked! "Shhhh! Hey, Babs. What's up? Here, catch!" She tosses her keys over the ledge where they land at Babs' feet. She doesn't even try to catch them. Babs bends to pick up the keys and sees something sparkle in the street just off the sidewalk. She crabwalks over to see what it might be and reaches in with one hand to stir through the gutter debris. Gum wrappers, a bottle cap, cigarette butts, muck. Then aha! There it is- the thing that caught her eye. It's a silver hoop earring, the kind that attaches with a backing, half submerged in the dirt, mud and other trash. Babs picks it up carefully, peering around for its mate or anything else shiny. She wipes off what she can with her free hand, transferring muck from the earring onto her fingers.

Satisfied, Babs crabwalks back to where the keys lay, picks them up and lets herself into Carla's building. She closes the door quietly behind her, making sure she hears the light 'click' of the latch. Someone broke into Carla's place a few months ago. The downstairs door doesn't lock if you don't pull on it. They walked upstairs and into her apartment, terrifying Carla even though they didn't touch her. She'd cowered in a corner while they tore through her shelves, looking for something to steal. But Carla collects old things and junk. The only thing of any real value in her apartment was her camera and her stash, neither of which the intruder found. In the end, he grabbed a bleached miniature skull Carla used as a bookend, causing the books to topple over. The cascade frightened the burglar off, leaving Carla breathless and excited, though she only told her friends about the break-in, not about how much she liked it.

Carla's landlady lives in the downstairs apartment, privately tucked behind the narrow stairwell. The stairs creak unless you step on the outer edges of the treads, which Babs does, tiptoeing her way up to the second floor.

At the top of the stairs, she turns left and unlocks Carla's door. The door to the right is a storage closet. Babs had inspected it one night while hanging with Carla and a group of other punks a month ago? A year? Everyone else had tried to find their way to the roof, and Babs had paused at this other door, curious what treasures it might hold. She'd jiggled and worried at the doorknob until something gave. The door had pulled open, revealing a closet stuffed full of stiff mopheads, dusty brooms, cans of cleaning solvent and paint, dirty rags, and boxes of brochures for some long-defunct food supply company. Nothing fun, nothing she wanted.

Babs lets herself into Carla's place quickly now, careful not to jangle the keys and wake the landlady below. Carla is just shutting up her Murphy bed, pushing it into place in the wall. Babs looks around. Carla has redecorated since the last time she was here. Everything is white- the walls, floor, fixtures- even the books seem to have been whitewashed. Babs can still read the titles but beneath a pale white haze across each spine. White gauze hangs in drifts and folds from the ceiling, creating waves that undulate in the slight breeze from the open window. Carla has obviously been up all night, probably cleaning. The apartment smells stoutly of lemon and soap.

"Babs, what brings you to my den of iniquity so early in the day?" Carla asks. She's standing awkwardly, with her hands on her hips and her elbows jutting forward at odd angles. "Or should I say late?" She licks her lips and smiles. Babs gets it. Carla is high. She looks around for someplace to sit, but there isn't any furniture except for a lone, white-washed trunk butted up against the front wall. Half-burnt candles line the front lip of the trunk, wax pooling around their bases. Babs holds out both hands- one with Carla's keys, and other offering the hoop earring from the street below. Carla takes her keys, and tentatively touches the earring. "You brought me... this?"

Babs snorts and tries to brush more scree from the hoop. "No, ha. I found this downstairs. Is it yours?"

Carla bites her lip. She has indeed been cleaning most of the night and doesn't like the sight of gunk flaking off the earring not only into Babs' hand, but some specks falling to the floor. She hangs her keys on the hook by her door, and says, "Wait a sec. Don't move." Babs stands still, holding the earring in her open palm, as Carla rushes to her sparkling kitchen at the back of the apartment and returns quickly with a small milky white ashtray. "Here. Put it here." Babs does, and Carla looks at the earring more closely. "Nope, not mine. If you don't want it, I'll do something with it..." She squats down, licks one finger, and picks up the tiny bits of dirt Babs has brought with her into the apartment.

Carla brightens. "Hey! You want to take a shower? I just got some new French rose soap that is so amazing! No offense but..." she wrinkles her nose. Babs gasps in mock horror. She lifts one arm first, then the other, and inhales deeply at each pit. Oh yeah... she's ripe. She should have thought of that before coming over. Babs knows Carla likes things so clean they're antiseptic. She thinks a second, why not? She could use a shower. The rose soap sounds nice. And once clean, she and Carla can get high and talk biz.

"Sure. That sounds nice. I've never used French soap before, I don't think..." She takes a step towards the bathroom, just to the left of the apartment door.

"Or I have some orange water soap too. You might like that." Carla sniffs at the air and decides that will pair best with the current scent of her place. "Yeah, that's better. It's French too." She steps into the small bathroom with its narrow shower stall, pedestal sink and toilet. Everything is white, framed by tiny octagonal floor tiles and beadboard with a slim shelf that runs the perimeter of the wall. White figurines, clear glass bottles, and multiple pairs of white die line the shelf. Babs can hardly wait to inspect each little thing once she's alone. Carla reaches into the small built-in cabinet just to the left of the shower stall and grabs a big white towel. It's very, very clean. She rummages through the one drawer of the cabinet until she finds what she is looking for, and hands Babs the towel and a brand-new bar of Savon de Marseillais. The wrapper seal is unbroken, with pretty orange and white stenciled flowers in a heavy black border.

Babs says, "Cool, thank you. I'll be right out." She takes the towel and soap, and Carla shuts the bathroom door for her. She spins around, trying to figure out what to do first. She wants to inspect all the pretty little things on the shelf. She wants to take a shower. She needs to unwind the strips of gauze at her legs, but there isn't much space in the small room, so she puts the towel down on the toilet seat lid and picks up a small white figurine of an angel, with its long wings and both arms extended as though asking for a favor or a hug. Ooo, Babs wonders if the angels she could almost see from the bus looked like this. She thinks maybe they did.

She puts the angel back in its place and strips down. Shoes first, then her ewwww rancid socks. Carla's not going to appreciate that. Next, Babs unwinds her gauze strip leggings, then pulls her culottes down. She layers the clothes on the floor- shoes first, then rancid socks, rolled up gauze strips, culottes on top. Last, she pulls her stinky though not rancid sleeveless t-shirt off and drops that in a pile on top of the rest of her clothes. She winks at the angel. "No peeking!"

As Babs begins to carefully unwrap the soap, the strains of Patti Smith's 'Horses' sounds out from the other room. 'Johnny something something something Johnny something something something'. Babs loves this song, but she never bothered to learn any of the lyrics. At the top, it's mostly spoken blah blah blah, though in a rocking chair cadence, perfect to play while you're getting high. She'll ask Carla to play it again when she brings out this clean new speed. Carla is going to love it. Babs sure hopes Carla will lend her the money.

3

Babs showers, firmly holding onto the brand-new bar of honeysuckle and orange-scented soap as she runs it all over her body. It's a little weird, feeling the soap press into her ribs, hipbones, and spare breasts. Like a washboard or cheese grater, Babs imagines soap flakes peeling off the bar as she runs it up and down her ribs and hips, breasts and belly. She has to lean against the wall of the shower stall to scrub at her stinky feet. Then she sits in the tiny stall and washes her legs, between her legs, her neck and arms. Carla was right. This soap is amazing.

She finishes soaping up, and turning this way and that, allows the hot water to cascade over her. Feeling luminous and clean, Babs turns off the water and opens the shower door in search of someplace to put the soap. She places the lathered bar on the edge of the sink, notices a small trickle of liquid bubbles oozing down into the bowl of the sink, and thinks 'oh Carla's not going to like that.' So she rinses the soap off and puts it back. It dribbles some more. She rinses it again, shakes it a few times over the sink, and places it back on the soap ridges. It dribbles. Babs mumbles "fuck!" under her breath and picks up the soap with the towel. She wipes the dribbles off the sink bowl, dabs at the soap bar with the towel, and places it back on the sink. No dribbles, good.

Carla knocks on the door. "Babs? Hey, I have something clean for you to wear, if you want..." Babs can hear the distress and longing in Carla's voice. As much as she really wants to put her gauze leggings back on, it would be best for her to change into something clean for Carla. She wraps the towel around her body and cracks the door. "Great, thanks," she stresses the thanks. She really wants Carla to be in a happy, giving mood. Carla hands Babs a stack of something white- of course, Babs thinks- and closes the door. "I'm making jasmine tea!" she calls out. "Ok, thanks!" Babs replies. She wipes the mirror of condensation- just a swipe to see her face. She wants to be sure she looks as clean as she feels. Oh shit! She realizes. It's all steamy in here! What if the speed got wet?

Babs starts to reach into her culottes to check on the speed and stops, thinking she should check it in the main room, where it's not all steamed up. She quickly dries off, and cracking the door ajar, unfolds a lacy white cotton slip sort of thing and a heavier white cotton muumuu of some kind, with light blue floral tracings around a slit at the neck. She drops the towel, puts the muumuu on the toilet seat, and pulls the cotton slip down over her head and arms. It falls to just above her knees, and is almost transparent with a tiny ridge of lace at the neck, arm holes and the bottom hem. It feels old, but well-preserved and soft. Babs guesses this might be an antique of some kind? She feels almost naked and though appreciates the second option.

She unfolds that- this is like her birthday with all these little gifts! Even if they're not hers, she's grateful to Carla for being so thorough. It seems like a good way to start this adventure. Unfolded, the muumuu turns out to have long sleeves and is cut very square with rectangles for arms and a rectangular long bodice. It's all white, of course, except for the tiny blue flowers stitched around the collar from neck to sternum. What is this thing called? She'll ask Carla about that and the angels she nearly saw. Gathering her dirty clothes, she steps out of the bathroom into the softly lit front room.

Carla is in the kitchen, so Babs call out to her, holding her clothes away from her oh so clean self. "Do you have a bag or something I can put these in?" She nudges at the socks with one thumb. "And I can chuck these. Ick."

Carla turns and opens a drawer. She rifles through a stack of neatly folded-by-size paper grocery bags and passes Babs a crisp large bag for her things. She grabs a smaller bag, snaps it open, and holds that out for Babs to deposit her decaying socks. As Babs dumps her things into the two bags, she notices that Carla is wearing another antique-y white slip-type thing. She studies the lacey plunging neckline and ruffles and notes that what Carla is wearing is more like a shorts-slip or slip-shorts, whatever you would call them: like a jumpsuit for a child, but with lace and ruffles, not ducks or kittens. She looks down at what she is wearing and pointedly at Carla's get up. "Where did you find these slip things? They're cool."

Carla grins broadly. "I've been hitting a lot of vintage stores and found this huge box of all these amazing turn of the century lace and filigree underwear. I got some beautiful cloche hats and some boots too, but tiny tiny tiny. Some of the lacey underwear I can't figure out. But they're gorgeous, either way. The slip you're wearing is way too small for me, so you can keep that if you want. The kaftan I'll want back though." She looks at Babs' clean bare feet. "Maybe you could check out the boots too? Though they might be too bitsy even for you."

Babs looks down and touches the thick cotton robe. "Oh this is a kaftan, cool. I thought it was a muumuu. Yeah, let's see the boots."

"First, let's have some tea. And tell me why you're here so early. Or late." She simpers and reaches past Babs to the stove to pick up two nested teacups and a steaming teapot. Not unlike Carla, the cups and teapot are dainty, the cups nearly translucent. She says, "Let's go hang in the balcony

room. I need a cig. This is jasmine tea. It's my new favorite."
Babs rolls up both paper bags, and as they pass the front door,
she drops them both on the floor. She remembers why she's
here, unrolls the larger bag and pulls the small packet of speed
from her pants pocket. It's dry, phew. She re-rolls the top of
the bag and follows Carla into a tiny room next to the front
door that leads out onto the balcony. It always seems more
like a closet with a balcony to Babs. It's Carla's favorite room.
They both sit with their backs against the inner wall as Carla
pours tea into the dainty cups and hands one to Babs. She
chews her lower lip and waits, watching to see what Babs
thinks of her new favorite tea.

Babs blows on the tea and takes a tentative sip. It smells like
those cigarettes Annie X is always smoking. And ow! It's
hot! She blows and sips again. The tea's a little tart- or
sour- her tastebuds are always shot unless something is
sugary sweet when she's high. She sips again, and says,
"It's kind of like flowers. I like it." She puts the teacup
down on the floor and holds the small envelope out to Carla
as an offering. "I also brought you something."

Carla squeals and picks the envelope up with spidery thin
fingers. She has bought speed from Babs plenty of times-
at shows, sometimes at parties when they run into one
another. They've never had any sort of formal seller-
buyer relationship though. Not like with Shelly or Annie

X. When Carla sees Shelly or Annie X, it's only ever to buy meth from them and nothing more. Carla always feels lucky that she isn't Annie X' type, so it's easy for them to do that 'here to buy then go' interaction. Carla is so excited about this unexpected gift, she has forgotten about the tea.

Babs adds, "I'd like you to try it out. I snorted some this morning and thought that was the shit. I'd like to see what you think, shooting it up." Carla licks her lips. "And then I have a favor to ask you, related."

Carla says, "Ok let me go set up my works. Do you have anything? Or do you need to borrow mine?" She stands and pauses at the doorway. Babs looks up, she feels so clean! "I came straight here from someplace else, so yeah, I didn't have time to grab my kit. Is your needle pretty sharp?" She has weak veins and hates poking around trying to find a good one. Carla nods, yeah she knows. "I do. And you know I clean my rig thoroughly. Let me set that up. Be ready in a jif." Carla runs off to the kitchen, pauses in the main room as though remembering something, and replaces Patti Smith with David Bowie's 'Aladdin Sane'. The first notes of 'Watch That Man' plonk out of the speakers set at opposite ends of the Murphy Bed-flanked bookshelves, perfect for getting high on this bright, grey Monday..? Tuesday? Morning.

As Carla sets things up in the kitchen, Babs sips at her tea and sings quietly along with the song. Carla left her cigarettes on the floor by the teapot, so Babs grabs the pack and shakes one out. "Can I have a cig?" She calls out. Carla replies, "Yeah sure, but let's do this first, then have one!" Babs can hear the excitement in Carla's voice. That girl probably likes to shoot speed more than anyone else Babs knows. And that's saying a LOT. Babs tucks the cigarette behind one ear, takes a sip of her tea- she does like it- and walks quietly back to the kitchen where Carla has almost completely set everything out just so. Kit unrolled off to the side, spoon set perpendicular to the sink, capped rig resting so many inches next to that, speed in its place of honor a few inches away from everything else. Carla's set up reminds Babs of the way her grandmother used to set the table- soup spoon, teaspoon, knife, main course fork, salad fork- all just so.

Carla gently opens the envelope, tapping it slightly on the left and on the right as she opens it to condense any loose crystals back into the main fold of the packet. No need, thinks Babs. This stuff is just one or two main rocks that will need to be chipped up or used whole. They're so fresh from the lab, no-one has had a chance to cut them. She can't believe she's going to be selling this shit! She's going to be so popular, so rich. Babs' mouth starts to water as she concentrates on Carla's every move. Carla gasps as she opens the envelope all the way, "Wow! What is this?! Where did you get it? It's so pretty..." The meth is glimmering, and Babs didn't notice this before. It's tinted pale green. So pretty...

Carla sets up the shot and offers it to Babs, who declines, saying, "No, I want you to try it first." But quickly, please. Babs is jonesing for a taste of this by needle. Her field of vision narrows to the works on the countertop. Carla does her shot, followed immediately by that terrific short cough– like a forced chemical blast that explodes from the back of your throat. Babs wants to know what Carla thinks. She wants to know what Carla is feeling. She wants to take her shot now too. Carla's hands shake slightly as she rinses the rig, then hands it to Babs, who takes her shot from what remains in the spoon. Carla had fixed up the smaller of the two rocks, so there's plenty left for an aftertaste later on.

Babs coughs and squeezes her eyes shut. She loves this part– the rush through her veins, behind her eyes, at the back of her head. She wishes she had thought to ask Carla to put 'Horses' back on, but the speedy chaos of 'Panic in Detroit' is fine for now. Ooo she knows what she wants to hear. She waits for Carla to clean everything up and pack her kit away, just so. She picks up her teacup and sips at it. Now it's cold and a little bitter. She puts the teacup back down, wanders into the main room and starts flipping through the records leaning against the wall. She finds what she was looking for- she knew she would!

"Hey Carla, I'm going to change the record, ok? Some Bauhaus?"

Carla calls out, "Sure. Then let's have that cig."

Babs lifts the needle before 'Cracked Actor' can start playing, and after sleeving the album, puts on the Bauhaus EP. She can't remember if she needs to switch the speed, so she waits until the music starts playing before deciding 'that sounds right' as the lovely first tap-tap-tapping devolves into echoes of tapping and one ringing bass note, again, and then again... She pulls the cigarette from behind her ear and goes into the balcony closet room to light up.

Gah, it's so bright now. Even with the soft grey fog limning the streets outside, the way the light is refracting off the white white walls of Carla's apartment, it hurts her eyes. Babs realizes she doesn't have her shades with her. Fuck! She didn't bring anything she needed! She rushes over to her bag of clothes, pulls out one of the rolls of gauze, and using her teeth, nips off a length of about two feet. As she settles down in the balcony closet again, back jammed against the inner wall and legs straight out facing the balcony, she loops the gauze strip lightly once, twice and three times around her head and over her eyes. Ah... that will do it.

Carla sits down beside her and laughs. "That's new. Can you see anything?" Babs swallows, she wishes she had a Slurpee right now. "No, but the light is too bright and I don't have my shades." She turns towards Carla, though she can't see her. "This works." Carla nods, cool. She moves the teapot and her forgotten teacup out of the way. She lights her own cigarette and then Babs'. They face the balcony and blow streams of smoke towards the open door.

"So... I think this is really good shit." Babs starts. "What do you think?" Carla exhales and licks her lips. "This is the cleanest speed I've had in a long, long time. Can you tell me where you got it?"

Babs almost tells her, but reins herself in. Whew, she's so high. This stuff is amazing. But when she's this high, there is no gap between what she thinks and what she says. It all comes blurting out of her, and she can't do that right now. "That's what I wanted to talk with you about. The guy- the people- who make this have asked me to be their... distributor? I guess, in the scene." Carla says, "Oh wow... the people who asked you... from the lab that makes this?" Babs nods, "Yeah, exactly. Just me. They only want one person to sell for them. They want me to pick up a big batch later tonight. But I need to get the money for the first batch somehow. So…"

"So you thought of me."

Babs presses her lips together. She can't see Carla's face, so she hopes Carla's not upset. "Well, yeah. But here's the deal. I get an excellent price. And for what I am picking up tonight, I can turn that around in a day and have your money back to you by tomorrow night. Plus, I will always hold some for you." She hopes she is being convincing enough. She's telling the truth, but she's a liar and people know that. There was the month she went around telling everyone she used to live at the Chelsea in New York and used to hang out with all those early punk icons: Sid and Nancy, Patti Smith, Richard Void, Debbie Harry… She embellished those lies with more made-up adventures- things she had done, people she had known, places she had been. The lies mounted one on top of the other until some punkette's cousin who was in town visiting actually had spent a lot of time at the Chelsea during those days. At a party, when the punkette introduced Babs as 'that girl who also lived at the Chelsea', the cousin pointed out that Babs was way too young to have been part of that scene and quietly suggested she stop spreading those lies.

She'd been so embarrassed by that episode, she'd begun

trying to tell the truth in earnest, though sometimes lies just slip out of her mouth, especially when she's high. So she concentrates on sounding like she's telling truth, even when she really is. "I mean, they told me they will always make this particular recipe. No changes. Did you know they use recipes?! And I will be the only dealer selling it in town. Well, they have someone else selling to the bikers and those folks. But no-one else in our scene. So if you can loan me the money for this first batch, I will always check in with you to see if you need any first."

Carla interrupts. "Like an investment." She knows a little about that sort of thing. "Yeah, cool. I like that." She realizes Babs can't see the smile on her face, so she nudges her. "I'm glad you thought of me. So, how much do you need for this first batch?"

Babs smiles hard. Carla said yes! "Do you have three thousand, seven hundred and fifty dollars? Or can you get that today? It's for a whole quarter."

Carla sucks in, "Whew! Hm, yeah I guess that makes sense. Yeah, I need to go to the bank to get that. When do you need it by?"

Babs lifts one corner of the gauze from her eyes and squints at Carla. "Oh my God Carla, this is going to be amazing.

Thank you!!" She drops the gauze back into place, closing her eyes again against the bright, hazy light. "I'm supposed to meet them tonight at, um, ten? Eleven? Shit, I think eleven. I'd better start writing this stuff down." She thinks, "And there's a show tomorrow at the Mab I can hit up. Plus I was thinking about going over to Jenn's house. Did you know her son Craig is in the Toiling Midgets?! I had no idea… but she's always looking to score, so I'm thinking I can sell some quantity there."

Carla gets up to put the record back on - might as well listen to this song again. She comes back and takes a sip of her cold tea. It's bitter, but Carla believes tea feeds you the flavor you deserve in the moment. She'll finish this cup, and follow it up with a fresh pot, hot and fragrant, not bitter at all. "Ok, the bank opens at nine. What time is it?" Babs shrugs. "Well, let's find out what time it is, then I can head over there. It's just up the street. You can stay here if you like, or come with, but I'll give you the money here." She pauses. "Is there something you can give me as collateral?" Carla peeks around the corner to the two rolled up paper bags by the door. "Anything back at your place?"

Babs thinks about it. "No… I had a good record collection, but Annie took that for rent last month. All I have is a bunch of, I don't know… I don't think stuff you would want." Babs is thinking of her black candles and the Crowley tarot desk she prizes that Annie hasn't taken from her yet. She also has a few pieces she uses in her every now-and-then magic spell castings- a painting of a unicursal hexagram Val traded her for speed once, a grimoire sort-of handbook printed by some local press, a small brass dish of salt, and a brass bell. Her chalice and crystals had been appropriated by Annie, so Babs has begun to hide the rest of her belongings in a small makeup kit wedged up into the chimney in her room.

Carla seems to be waiting for more, so Babs says, "You know, my black magic things. Black candles, stuff like that. I don't think you'd want any of that here."

"Ah, right. Don't suppose any of those things are white? Like white magic?"

"Nope, sorry. I could give you my grimoire to hold onto if you like. That's the spellbook?" Babs is thinking of all the books Carla likes to collect. Carla ponders that. "No... it's ok. You stay here, I'll get the money. Then we can... ooooh! I got it!" Carla jumps a little, what a perfect idea. "You do all that magic stuff. What if we do a white magic blood ceremony? I read about this somewhere, in one of my books." She jumps up and runs over to the Murphy bed shelves. After a few minutes of scanning titles, she pulls one book from the shelf and brings it over to Babs.

"This book, it talks about white magic, and there is something about a blood spell. To bind us? In an agreement?" Carla flips through the pages of the book. "It's here somewhere... hah! This says all we need is a candle, and to mix a few drops of our blood into the flame together. Oh, and we need some sandalwood, and bay leaves. Basil too. I have some sandalwood incense. And can pick up some bay leaves and basil at the Chinese market on my way back from the bank!"

Babs is impressed. She has worked on casting spells for the past year, but always on her own, alone in her room at Annie X's. She's never thought to cast a spell with someone by her side, though she supposes that would be what witches in a coven do. The idea of mixing her blood with Carla's makes her a little nervous. But hell, they share blood when they share needles, which they've done plenty of times. So they're already linked anyway, in a way. Why not? And she reminds herself, it's just for this one loan. Then everything will be behind them, the spell completed. "That's a great idea."

Carla jumps up and runs to the kitchen to check on the time. They have hours before the bank opens, so she makes some more tea and they hang out, changing records and smoking while Babs tells Carla about the bat cave and her other plans. She asks about the angels she almost saw, and the small porcelain angel in Carla's bathroom. She mentions running into Steph and the Brotherhood of Night-Light that Steph is learning how to run. She doesn't say anything about Ed being the source of the speed. She has to keep some secrets...

Carla corrects her, "I think it's just Brotherhood of Light. Didn't they do something out at that show in East Bay?" Oh right, Brotherhood of Light. Babs likes Brotherhood of Night-Light better. Or better yet, Sisterhood of Night Light. It reminds her of vampires, which for some reason, she feels connected to. Carla pulls out her camera and takes a few photos of Babs in her gauze blindfold, smoking and drinking tea. Babs thinks about the Sisterhood of Night Light and if she should get some kind of old timey sign referring to their name, like a shingle in an actual office, in the house she is going to paint black.

"I have seen purer liquors, better segars, finer tobacco, truer guns and pistols, larger dirks and bowie knives, and prettier courtesans here in San Francisco than in any other place I have ever visited; and it is my unbiased opinion that California can and does furnish the best bad things that are available in America."
— **Hinton Helper**

Give Me That

1

"Even if she's not home, we can just hang out and wait for her. I do that all the time. If Craig is here, we can find out what's going on with Gabe, huh...?" Babs pokes Carla in the upper arm with two fingers, teasing her about this new thing that might be going on between her and Gabe. Babs didn't feel confident about managing her first large sale on her own, so she'd asked Carla to come with her to Jenn's apartment up on Golden Gate. Babs needs Carla's backbone, as fragile as it may be. She's worried about how Annie X might take Babs branching out onto her own, selling meth at large in the punk community. She's seen what Annie can do- violently swinging her baseball bat around, or just as scary, using her bulk and fury to frighten punks into submission. Annie likes Carla, so maybe if she hears that Carla is somehow tied up in this new adventure, she'll back off and leave Babs alone.

The previous day, Carla had gone to the bank and returned with the cash. Then Babs and Carla performed a white magic blood ceremony. They'd each pricked one finger, intermingled drops of their blood at the base of a white candle, and burned basil and bay leaves as they simultaneously lit the candle and a stick of sandalwood incense. Carla's book of white magic told them to repeat their desires three times. Babs added a bit of her own magical knowledge and had them repeat "Gifts gifts, come to we. With this spell, we set you free. Flow into our life at ease. Abundance now, eternally." They'd stumbled over the words on the third repetition and dissolved into a fit of giggles. For good measure, they'd sucked a taste of blood from the tips of each other's fingers. That seemed like the right thing to do. Both Babs and Carla felt confident about this business deal, though Babs calls it their adventure.

After they watched the candle burn for a minute and nothing happened, the two meandered across the apartment, each in her own world. Babs scratched out copious notes, convoluted diagrams, and intricate budgets and lists for her new business. In her mind, the plan was concrete: she would sell a lot of speed, get an apartment, decorate it, set up an office, and call her business either the Sisterhood of Night Light or the Batcave. She can't decide between the two and knows satori will strike when the time is right to decide upon the name.

Carla had scrubbed the bathroom, then messed around with her camera in between changing records and dancing around the apartment. By the time Babs called the taxi from the card Ed had given her, she was desperate to flee from the twentieth "Sex Bomb Baby" spin on the turntable. Babs likes Flipper, but enough is enough. If it had been Bauhaus, she might not have minded so much.

She made the pickup and set a date to go to some ranch Ed has outside the City to do target practice and learn some other stuff he says is important to know about guns. Then she stopped at the corner store to buy a Pepsi and a small notebook where she can keep track of appointments and record her income and expenses. Just like a real businesswoman! She stopped by her place, poked at her meager possessions, and called for Luna hoping her rat might show up. But not a peep from the rodent. Babs hopes Luna turns up before she moves out, whenever that happens.

She packed a change of clothes and returned to Carla's for the night. If she still had her board, she would have stashed everything at Carla's and skated up and down the streets of North Beach to feel the breeze along her arms and to ease the strain of the past few days. She's allowing herself to feel a little angry at Annie, now that she knows she won't have to live under the big blonde's threats much longer. That bitch had no right to take Babs' record collection and skateboard. That's something else she'll have to buy herself when all this money starts pouring in.

At Carla's, Babs recorded in her little book the things she would need to buy: (1) scale, cellophane baggies, tape, and teensy labels so she can scribble the weight of each bag in her tiny, precise handwriting. Oh, and she needs a really good pen.

Then she got to work. She scooped a small rock out of one of the four baggies Ed had handed over in exchange for all that moolah. The cash had seemed unreal, like toy money. But the meth! That was so real! She and Carla had done a small celebratory bump. They had to test the wares, after all, to make sure quality control was up to par, right? And oh boy, it was.

Babs was enjoying a high-pitched whistling in her ears when Carla handed her a black and red lacquered box inlaid with dragons and clouds across the top and all four sides. She said it was a safety deposit box or something like that. Babs thanked her and wondered to herself what else she was supposed to do for Carla besides get her high.

Once she placed the four baggies carefully in the box and admired it sitting there full of her dreams, Babs attacked her little notebook anew, re-writing her plans over and over again in her cramped, precise penmanship. She kept making mistakes though, and rather than scratch them out, she started the list over, tearing out page after page so everything was perfect. She'd get it right this time for sure...

As Babs scribbled away against Carla's trunk in the front room, she began to hallucinate little toy soldiers or nutcrackers – she couldn't quite figure out what they were- marching in circles around her. At first, they seemed friendly, but as they continued to parade about, they became threatening and aggressive. Babs realized, phew, she'd been awake for far too long. She needed a beer, but it was well after two in the morning, so nothing was open. With no respite in sight, she started freaking out a little. Her breath came in shallow, jagged bursts as she tried to stay cool. She didn't want the toy soldiers to know they were getting under her skin. Her vision blurred around the edges, and they kept marching.

Meanwhile, Carla had stepped out. As Babs was trying to figure out how to escape the little soldiers- or perhaps hide from them- the apartment door opened, and Carla returned, juggling two large paper bags. Arms and legs mid-swing, the soldiers froze in place and vanished. And oh, Carla had picked up supplies while out: soft white bread, sugar, cinnamon, butter, and a bottle of whiskey. Carla was her knight in shining white armor! Her sister of night light or knight light! Whatever she was, she was most definitely Babs' savior: for the loan, the new Sisterhood, the treats, and making the little soldiers disappear.

They'd made cinnamon toast and drunk almost the entire bottle of whiskey. It was good. Something Irish that Babs had never heard of before. That went into her little notebook as another thing she needed to buy for her apartment/office when the money came in. Eventually, Babs curled up in the tiny balcony room and fell asleep.

This morning, or today, whatever time they woke up, Carla made more of that jasmine tea for Babs, but she wanted one of those bittersweet coffee drinks from her favorite café down the street. After they took turns showering and getting ready to go out, they tripped downstairs and over to Caffe Trieste for lattes and gelato. There, they made plans to go to Jenn's place together to sell some speed.

First, they strolled up to the tiny headshop off Columbus where Carla helped Babs choose an impressive-looking pale green scale with all these cute little counter measure pieces. All the dealers she knows have scales, but this is the most sci-fi looking piece of equipment she's ever seen. Carla paid for it, along with the stacks of baggies and tiny labels Babs wanted and Babs wrote it all down in her notebook. She didn't want Carla to feel used, especially now that they were becoming friends? Partners? Night Light sisters. They'd returned to the apartment, where Carla set Babs up at her kitchen table and left her alone to divvy up the portions she would sell later on that night at the Mab.

So here they are, downstairs at Jenn's place. Babs rings the buzzer, and as they wait for someone to clomp down the stairs and let them in, Babs runs her hands over the hair on one side of her head. It's over an inch long– too long– and lying flat against her skull. She needs a buzz. Maybe tonight before the show, she can swing by Annie's to grab her clippers. They're dull, but they'll get the job done.

The door peels open, surprising Babs out of her thoughts. It's Craig! Babs can hardly wait to ask him about what his band is up to, what's happening, where he's been. Oh, and if he's talked to Gabe lately, and if he knows what Gabe is up to, and if he might get Gabe to come over while Carla is here too. So much to remember to do. It's a good thing she has her notebook and can keep track of it all.

Craig invites them upstairs. They follow him as Babs starts asking questions about the Toiling Midgets. How was their last tour, how long are they in town, where are they going next. As always, Carla has her camera, and snaps shots of

Craig's black jeans-clad legs as they hike up the stairs. Craig says his mom isn't there right now but should be right back, so they can wait with him, if they don't mind him changing his guitar strings. He can't believe they lasted the whole tour. They're completely un-tunable and need to be chucked.

At the top of the stairs, they enter a large living room with a high ceiling, fronted on one side by two bay windows overlooking Golden Gate Ave. The room is filled with frumpy overstuffed couches and armchairs set in a half circle around a wide copper-topped coffee table. The copper top is buried under a pizza box, guitar string packets, empty bottles of beer strewn everywhere, and a massive squat bong, bright red as a fire hydrant and reeking of skunk. That bong water really needs to be changed. Babs wrinkles her nose. Fucking hippies.

Craig's mom is a scion of San Francisco's hippie years. If you spend any time around her, you hear all her stories about the good old bad days with Jefferson Airplane, the Grateful Dead, Big Brother and the Holding Company, blah blah blah. Babs has heard all the stories plenty of times. She doesn't mind so much though. Jenn is a cool mom and totally supportive of Craig's music and all the kids in the punk scene. She never judges or lectures Babs when Babs buys speed from her, and instead, she sometimes makes her a peanut butter sandwich and invites her to watch TV and hang out. So Babs listens to the stories and shares her own. Most of the time, she thinks that they're all part of one long continuous tale set in San Francisco, the gorgeous entity she now considers their sister City of Night Light. The thought makes Babs smile.

But bleah, every now and then, when Babs is confronted with something like this stinky gross bong, or some long-haired gross hippie guy sprawls across the couch almost touching her- Babs doesn't like to be touched by hippies if she can help it- she recoils and remembers 'never trust a hippie', just like the song says.

Babs sits at the end of the couch closest to the stairwell, as far from the bong as possible. Carla sits in one of the dirty faux-velvet low-slung armchairs at the end of the room, nearest the windows. She snaps a few pictures of the debris on the table, of Craig's fingers as he unwinds strings from his guitar. Babs nervously plays with the strap of the leather purse Carla had lent her for the day. It's a funky little purse, no bigger than a couple of packs of cigarettes, with a tongue that inserts into a flat loop to keep it closed. The stitching that connects the shoulder strap to the purse is coming unraveled, so she plays with those bits, plucking and pulling at the frayed ends while they wait.

She wishes she had an excellent pen like she'd wanted to buy, but they'd had no time to stop by a stationary store before heading over here with a few quarters and dimes to sell as samples to Jenn. At the last minute, Babs had thrown a whole ounce divided into 4 baggies into the purse, just in case. You never know who you might run into and what they might need. Babs knows the pen is on her list, so she refrains from pulling out her little notebook to write it down again. She knows she'll lose herself in jot jot jot if she starts, so pick pick pick is better.

Babs and Craig talk about the scene and what's been happening in town while his band was on tour. They were only gone ten days, but there's always a lot to catch up on in the City of Night Light. Babs sees the words in capital letters in her head, maybe with lightbulbs writing out each letter like a marquis. She snaps back to the conversation she's having with Craig and asks if he's seen Gabe. Nope, he only just got home last night and hasn't had a chance to check in on his friend. She wishes she could do a line while they're waiting, but Craig doesn't do drugs. Not that he's uptight about his friends doing them. Hell, his mom deals drugs out of their home. He just doesn't partake. He says it affects his hearing, and he likes to stay present when he's playing, when he's with people, or doing whatever he does. Babs doesn't get it, but she likes Craig, so it's cool.

Craig finishes replacing his strings and tunes the guitar. It's a butterscotch blonde Fender Telly with a maple fingerboard, he explains to Babs. She nods and asks questions about what this part does, and what is that knob there. It's a pretty guitar she supposes, though not sparkly like the guitars she prefers. It has scratches gouged into it along the back. Babs points that out, and Craig lifts the guitar to show her the fat skull belt buckle he wears on his belt. That caused the scratches, like war wounds, he says.

The door downstairs opens and closes. Jenn calls out, "I'm home! Craig, are you hungry, honey?" She huffs up the stairs and pauses at the landing that leads into both the living area and the kitchen off to the right. She's carrying two large trays of something that smells tomatoey and spicy at once. The smell of food mixed with the rancid bong water makes Babs' stomach turn. She stands to greet Jenn.

2

"Hey Jenn! How are you?" She gestures to Craig, "Must be nice having him home." She smiles. Let's get past this blah de blah and onto business, she thinks, but she can't help it and starts yammering. Where ya been, whatchya doing, what's new. Jenn puts the trays of food into the fridge, carries her shapeless cloth hippie purse over to the living room and sits in the other armchair next to Carla. "Carla? Sweety, I haven't seen you in a very long time. I like all this," she twirls a hand in the air around Carla's face, like she's stirring something up. "You look so pale though. Have you always been this pale? I don't remember."

Carla snaps a shot of Jenn's fingers and replies, "Oh, I'm good. I've been kind of laying low, doing this," she lifts the camera, "and sorta staying in North Beach. I haven't been to the Haight or anywhere in awhile."

Babs sits down again and leans in, "Since that thing that happened over at Shelly's, you know? When Gabe got pistol-whipped?"

Craig strums his guitar and says," Yeah that bullshit. He's lucky he wasn't shot."

Carla adds, "I was there. I know. Some other girl who was

there- I don't remember who- drove him to the hospital in my car." She turns to Babs. "Was that you?"

Babs shakes her head no. "Nope, I wasn't there. But I came over later." She raises her eyebrows. "There was a scary vibe going on at Shelly's after that. Did you hear that someone paged her '666' then 'Emergency' and then '666' again from her house while it was happening?!"

Craig and Carla nod their heads, yup. Jenn says, "No! I didn't hear about that! Who called her?"

Babs chirps, "No-one knows. Spooky shit."

Jenn leans over and grabs the bong, sniffs at it, and clears a space for it on the table before her. "So... no one admits to calling? Or maybe someone called then left? Or...?"

Craig plucks a few strings and looks at his mom. "No, that's just it. No one at the house called her at all until after it was over, and Gabe was at the hospital already. Those pages came in while it was happening and from her house."

Jenn shivers, "Brrrrr.... That IS scary." She looks around and pats the shirt pockets on her faded denim shirt. "Craig, have you seen my weed anywhere?"

"Nope, I just got up a little while ago, and Carla and Babs buzzed right after. I haven't even had anything to eat yet. So whatever you brought, I might have some of that." He stands and looks around the room. "Did you look in Harvey?"

Jenn places a hand on each knee and pushes herself up to stand. "No, I didn't. Thanks, sweety." She crosses to the fireplace against the wall opposite the couch and removes the head off a large white porcelain rabbit. Reaching inside the rabbit's body, she pulls out a baggie of weed. "Voila! You're so good to your mom." She smiles at Craig.

Jenn returns to her seat and loads herself a bowl. Babs can't help but wrinkle her nose. Nasty bongwater, gross dope. Hopefully the gelato she ate this morning doesn't come up. The thought makes her gag just a little.

As Jenn pokes through the debris strewn across the coffee table in search of a lighter, she asks, "So girls, what brings you here today?" Babs looks at Carla. Carla looks at Babs. She shrugs her shoulders. Go, she gestures with both hands. Babs clears her throat. "Well, I actually came over because I have something you might want to check out." She grins and inserts one hand into her small leather stash.

Jenn stops looking for the lighter and looks surprised.

"Oh really? That's a first. Do you want to step into the other room?"

Babs glances at Craig and Carla. "No, that's ok. Carla knows. Craig can stay too, that's cool." But Jenn shakes her head no. "Actually, I'd rather not have Craig witness any transactions. I think it's better if he doesn't know the particulars of anything drug-related." She pauses, "It IS drug-related?"

Babs nods her head. "Oh yes... I think this is something you're really going to be interested in, too."

Jen pushes herself up to stand again and walks towards the kitchen and the small bedroom beyond. "Well then, come with me. Let's chat back here."

Babs gives Carla a look, asking is this okay? Carla waves her off and turns her attention to her camera, adjusting something on the lens. "It's fine. Craig and I can hang out."

Babs follows Jenn into the back room and Carla snaps a blurred shot of them as they leave. Craig lays his guitar along the length of the couch and leans across the coffee table towards Carla. "So you're still doing photography. Can I see whatchya got going on?"

Carla hesitates. She likes what she's heard about Craig though she doesn't know him personally all that well. Everyone says he's an honest guy, but it discomfits her letting other people handle her camera. Sure, if something bad happened, she could always get it fixed or buy another. But this Nikon has been her pal for years. Craig notices her hesitation and waves his hands, "No no, I get it. I feel the same way about Betsy," He places one hand on the body of his Telecaster. Carla notices a sticker of a small female figure at the base of the headstock, and she leans over to have a closer look.

"Can I...?" Craig knows what she's looking at. "Oh, Betsy, yeah!" Carla walks behind the couch for better light and takes a few shots of the figure. She's kneeling in a U.S. flag bathing suit, with one hand raised behind her head, tucked into her curly updo. Kind of like Wonder Woman, but blonde and blue-eyed. "That's Betsy, where I got the name for my guitar," he explains.

As Carla leans in to take another photo of Betsy and the tuning pegs, the downstairs buzzer rings, making her jump.

Craig laughs. "Yeah, that's loud." He starts for the stairwell. "We keep trying to figure out how to turn it down, but whatever we do shuts it off. So, it's either really on or totally off." He pauses at the top of the stairs, "Be right back."

He clomps down the stairs- even barefoot, Craig walks like

he's in his Doc Martin's - speaks with someone at the door, and comes back up, followed by two greasy, long-haired hippies. One is short and overweight, wearing small wire-rimmed granny glasses and a creamy white Irish crewneck sweater and ripped jeans. He has a full beard that makes his face look rounder than it probably is. The other hippie is much bigger all around- taller and wider across the arms and chest- and is wearing a jeans jacket with the arms cut off, a black t-shirt with wings imprinted on the front, and ripped jeans too. His beard is shorter than the other hippie's beard. Carla figures he's a biker and avoids looking at him.

Craig grabs his Telly and leans it against the wall behind the couch. He tells the hippie/biker duo, "Go ahead and have a seat. Jenn will be out in a sec." Hey, he calls his mom by her first name, thinks Carla. I never noticed that before.

The two sit on the couch where Craig and Babs had been sitting minutes before. The hippie leans over, grabs the bong and bag of weed Jenn had left out and takes a whiff. He clears a new space for them on the coffee table in front of him. The biker opens the pizza box, and finding it empty, moves it to the floor at the end of the couch.

"Go for it, J," the biker grumbles. His voice is gravelly like sandpaper, though deep and rich, not light and scratchy as

Carla imagines sandpaper would sound. She fiddles with her f-stop. The hippie- I guess Jay? She thinks - packs more weed into the bowl, takes the proffered lighter from the biker, and sucks in a long, gurgling hit. Carla grimaces slightly at the fusty stank burbling into the room. When Jay exhales, Craig cracks a window, and after a beat, opens it further. "Shit, that bong needs to be cleaned. You want me to find you a pipe or something else?"

Hippie Jay shakes his head no. No-name-yet biker takes the bong, sniffs it, and says, "It's alright. We just gotta see Jenn about something and we'll be gone." He hands the bong back to Jay. Carla snaps a shot of the bong being passed hand to hand, with just a whisper of beard fuzzily in play behind the bong and hands in focus. Click whir click whir. No-name-yet biker raises his gaze to Carla and says, "Give me that." He holds one hand out towards Carla's camera. She grasps it a little tighter, reflexively. "It's a Nikon. See?" She holds it up from her lap slightly, placing her other hand protectively on top of the lens. No-name-yet growls, "I mean Give. Me. That. You can't take any pictures here."

Carla looks at Craig, inquisitively. "Craig? Really? Jenn's been fine with it." Her heart speeds up. She's a little scared of no-name-yet. Craig moves next to Carla. "It's cool, man." He says directly to no-name-yet. The biker stands up and reaches across Jay towards the camera. "Nope. It isn't cool. Give me that. Or gimme the film. Just take it out and give it to me." Carla swallows dryly. Her heart is fluttering against her chest and her knees feel watery.

Craig calls out, "Hey mom! Jenn! Can you come out here, please?! We've got kind of something going on! We need you out here!" He starts to step away from Carla's side, then thinks twice and stays put.

At odds with the tension in the room, hippie Jay's demeanor is suuuuper laid back. He seems to be vaguely gazing at something hovering over the coffee table, unfazed by no-name-yet's aggression. Carla realizes he hasn't said a word since they arrived. Can he talk? What's going on here? She turns her attention back to the biker, whose anger only seems to be escalating. Suddenly, she has to pee.

No-name-yet raises his voice, "I'm not fucking around. Give me your camera. Now." Craig raises his voice too. "Jenn! Get out here!!" The door off the kitchen flies open and Jenn rushes past the kitchen into the living area. She takes in the scene: Craig protectively standing between Carla and the two at the couch, no-name-yet biker leaning over the coffee table as he reaches for Carla's camera, and hippie Jay staring off at nothing through his granny glasses.

"Ok. Danny, please sit down. And somebody tell me what's going on." When Danny doesn't sit, Jenn repeats herself, "Danny, please. Sit down." She looks at Craig. "Honey? What happened?"

Craig doesn't take his eyes off Danny. "I don't know, Jenn. This guy just... suddenly freaked out. This one," he points at hippie Jay, "...took a bong hit. Carla was taking some pictures like she always does. And that one," he points at Danny who has perched himself on the couch, "started telling her to give him her camera."

Danny growls, "You know I can't let any photos get taken of ..." He jerks his head at hippie Jay. Carla looks at hippie Jay again. What the hell is happening? Babs steps quietly into the kitchen, nervously taking in what's unfolding in the other room. Carla tries to catch her eye, but Babs is looking at hippie Jay and Danny.

Jenn walks around the coffee table and plants her feet across from Danny and hippie Jay. To ease the energy, she clasps her hands behind her back. "Ok. I understand what's going on." She faces Carla. "Carla, sweety, you can't take any pictures of my guest here," she nods her head towards hippie Jay. "Do you have film in your camera?"

Carla relaxes and she doesn't need to pee so bad. She looks

up at Craig, then around the room at hippie Jay, Danny, and Babs, finally settling her gaze upon Jenn. "I do. But Jenn, I never take pictures of anyone's face without asking them first. You've seen my photos. Everything is unfocused except one item and that's never anyone's face. You know...? I promise you, I only took shots of their hands, no faces at all."

"Bullshit!" Danny barks at Carla. But he looks at Jenn. "That's bullshit. I need her to give me that film."

Jenn raises one hand as though stopping traffic. "Danny, I know Carla's pictures, and she means what she said. They're all fuzzy, with one thing in focus. If she says she only took pictures of your hands, then I believe her." She looks at Carla again. "You promise there are no pictures of anyone's face, sweety?"

Carla nods emphatically. "I promise. And I'm not just saying that." She tells Danny, "If you've ever been to the Telegraph Hill Postcard Shop, they carry a series of my photos." The look on his face tells her he has no idea what she's talking about. "I'm almost at the end of my roll of film. Otherwise, I would give it to you. But please, I swear, I didn't take pictures of any faces." She shakes her head. "Please don't take my film or my camera."

Danny relaxes. Oh my God, Carla thinks, does he believe

me? Even though she is telling the truth, she didn't think he would listen. He leans an elbow on each knee. "Alright. If you say so, Jenn. And Carla. Hmm. Ok. But if I hear about any photos from this..." he waves his fingers around at the room, "I'm gonna come find you."

Jenn touches Carla lightly on the shoulder. "Carla, if you promise me, then I believe you. Why don't you and Babs head home, and let me see to my other guests' needs."

Carla looks over at Babs, bouncing on her feet nervously by the stairwell. "Babs...?"

"Yeah, we're good to go." She waves at Craig, "Bye Craig. Tell Gabe Carla and me say hi." She starts to say something to the men on the couch, then decides 'nah' and beckons to Carla. "Let's go. Thanks, Jenn. I'll check in with you in a couple of days, ok?"

Jenn smiles and says, "Sure thing, sweety". Carla glances at hippie Jay who doesn't seem to have noticed any of what just occurred. Carla's knees are still shaky, so she wobbles over to Jenn for a brief hug, whispers "Thank you," and pauses at the stairwell, waiting for Babs to finish up.

Babs whispers over her shoulder, "Say goodbye to Craig."

Carla furrows her brow. Didn't she already...? "Bye Craig." She takes the stairs and waits down below for Babs to follow.

Once the door is shut behind them, they both exhale. "Whew!!!" Carla leads them briskly up Golden Gate towards Divisadero. "What the hell was that?!" Babs chuckles, at first to herself, then louder. She grabs Carla by the arm and pulls her, moving them further away from the house.

3

"You have no idea who that was?" Babs looks at her friend gleefully. Carla shakes her head, no. They turn left on Divisadero towards the lower Haight and slow down. They are both thinking about heading home, but for each that is in a different direction. "Ok, so that..." Babs grins, "was Jerry Garcia. From the Grateful Dead?" Carla gasps. Babs explains, "That other guy was his body-guard or something. Larry told me he goes around with Hell's Angels as his personal body guards, or whatever you call it. That's why he wanted your camera! You were taking pictures of Jerry Garcia buying dope!"

Carla laughs nervously and her knees collapse then catch. She leans against a small wrought iron gate next to the building where they have stopped. "Oh my God. I took a picture of him smoking weed. Well, no, passing the bong. But..." she looks at Babs carefully. "That isn't so bad though. Pot? Come on..."

Babs shakes her head. "I don't think he was there to buy weed. I hear he has a little romance going with Hoodoo." Carla's mouth drops into a perfect 'O'. "Really?! I thought all those old hippie guys just smoked a lot of pot and do acid."

Babs pauses until a couple passes them on the sidewalk.

"Yeah, not what I hear. About Jerry Garcia, anyway. I don't really know any hippies. I mean, I sorta know some of the soup kitchen ones. And Jenn. But she's different. She does a little speed and smokes pot, and obviously, she sells heroin. But I don't think she partakes."

Carla thinks about this and nods. "Well shit, I'm just glad that Danny biker guy didn't grab my camera. Or worse." She shudders. Then she remembers, "Oh! Were you able to get everything done with Jenn?"

Babs pokes Carla lightly on the arm with two fingers. "Oh my God! She bought a whole ounce off of me! I knew it. I just knew it, so I brought extra, just in case."

Carla tilts her head to one side. "You brought an entire ounce of meth with you today? Just, on the bus?" She thinks a second. "And now you have... how much money?" She shakes her head and looks around. "Shouldn't we keep moving to get someplace safe?" Only one couple has passed close to them and they are on a busy street, but her knees suddenly go weak.

Babs looks down at the leather purse clasped tightly in her hand. "Yeah... maybe you're right." She feels a little light-headed. Time for another shot. She should get ready for the Mab and she needs to buzz her head. And get that pen. And pick up a paper to start looking at apartments. So much to do. She looks up the street, thinking of which way to go next. She can hoof it back to Annie X' place or grab a bus over on Haight.

She wraps her fingers around one of Carla's arms and pulls her up the brick stairs next to the gate Carla has been leaning against. They both sit, knees privately touching as they face one another on the stairs. She digs into the purse and pulls out a fat envelope bursting with cash. Carla watches nervously as Babs counts out thirty-eight one hundred-dollar bills and five ten-dollar bills. "Here. Plus one hundred for the scale. Count it again." She hands Carla the cash. Carla takes the money and tucking it between their bodies and the door behind them, starts to count it, stops, starts over. "That's it. It's all there. That's amazing." She widens her eyes at Babs and shoves the money into the satchel that holds her camera and extra rolls of film.

"Um... so now what? Are you coming back to my place? Your stuff is there." Babs shrugs. "Yeah, I know. I need to go back to Annie's and get some things. Get ready for the show tonight. Do you mind if I stop by later, on my way there? Probably around nine." Carla purses her lips in thought. "Actually, I was thinking I might dink around Coit, take some photos of the City tonight. Can you come a little earlier?" She muses, "I wish I had a spare key for you."

Babs smiles. Carla really is her sister of Night Light! "Sure, I can come I guess around 8:30? We can celebrate a little before you go do that and I go to the Mab." She looks up the street again, squinting. There's a bus that runs on Hayes, can she see it from here? When she gets her place, she'll have an extra key made just for Carla. That can be a stop-off for Carla when she's up in Babs' part of the City, since Babs thinks she'd like to stay around Haight, or maybe in the Castro somewhere. She'd like to get that paper and start looking now. Maybe she'll even have time to make some calls before tonight. How much will she need for an apartment? It's been so long since she's had to pay rent, she doesn't know how much it will cost. She remembers something about having to fill in applications, like getting a job. But oh shit, she doesn't have a job, so will she be able to find someone willing to rent to her? Well, first thing's first. Get a paper, and a good pen, and do a shot, and buzz her head, and have a smoke, and... shit, was that the bus?

She threads the small tongue into its loop on the purse, and making sure Carla has put her money away, stands up. "I'm gonna run and catch the bus. You ok from here?" Carla giggles. "Yes, mommy. I can get home all by my lonesome from here." Babs snorts. "Ha! Ok see ya later." She clips down the stairs and runs up towards Hayes, wishing she was on a skateboard, hearing the clackety-clack of its wheels on the sidewalk.

Babs misses the bus she thought she saw, but another one trundles along soon enough and drops her half a block from the corner store near Annie X. She grabs a paper and a pack of Bubble Yum, and miracle of miracles! They have not the best of pens, but one of her favorites– a fine point felt tip pen that won't bleed on the paper. She smirks as she thinks, 'Hallelujah, all praise the mighty corner store'. Paper bag crumpled in one hand, she speed-walks down the street to Annie X', and takes the stairs as quietly as she can, hoping to avoid Annie if possible. Much to do and no time to dally. Besides, if Annie sees Babs, she might remember she'd told her to get out by Sunday– what was that, a week ago? The day had come and gone with no repercussions. But just to be safe, Babs has been tiptoeing in and out of the squat to avoid a run-in with the big bitch.

At the entrance to her room, Babs checks for the scrap of cloth she'd left wedged in the latch. It isn't there, so she knows Annie has been snooping around her room again. She becomes flushed with anger that quickly turns to relief. At least Annie hasn't just chucked her few belongings onto the street.

Babs shuts the door to her wee room and calls out softly for Luna, but there's no sign of the tiny white rat. She meticulously displays her purchases across the hearth where she usually lays out her spells. She surveys the room, then tiptoes into the kitchen and quietly half-fills a jelly jar with water from the tap.

The next steps happen by rote: back to her room, close the door, lay out her shot, tie off, and weeeee... After that first sweet rush washes through her brain, Babs scans the Apartments For Rent section in the Haight and Castro. She circles the apartments that sound promising, wishing she had a phone in her room so she could call them all now. Rent is more than she thought it might be- Twelve hundred or so for two-bedroom apartments- but she calculates she should have enough for the first, last and deposit sometime later this week. Plus be able to buy more speed.

She goes over her budget notes again, decides to alter the numbers a little to allow for her own sips and sampling, and satisfied she'll still make a lot of fucking money, wonders where she should keep it. Can she open a bank account? Or get a safe? Where would she keep that before she can get her own place? As she pores over her newspaper and notes, she starts to shake and sweat. Ooo maybe she did a little too much. This stuff is really fucking good- so uncut and clean. She needs to remember to remind herself to shoot smaller amounts. She has to figure out the right balance with this shit to stay high but not jingly. She's a businesswoman now after all.

Her gut clinches, and she tiptoes quickly over to the bathroom. Ugh, since she'd eaten, the speed is trotting it right through her. Ick, shitting is so gross. She wishes she didn't have to eat, ever.

As her heart rate settles down to a rapid, steady thuh-thud thuh-thud, Babs grabs her clippers, slips back into the bathroom- now perfumed with her stink- and buzzes both sides of her head over a small paper bag propped up in the sink using the #2 guard. Short but not skull short. She wipes the clippers semi-clean with her fingers and tosses the bag of clippings into the trash. On second thought, she grabs the bag and tucks it inside her room. She shouldn't leave anything behind that Annie might have someone use to cast a spell on her. Better super safe than ultra sorry.

She knows it's much too early to head back over to Carla's yet- she has hours to go- so Babs sorts through her meager belongings. She sorts her small pile of shirts, pants and underwear. She lines up her clippers, miscellaneous jotted spells, notes, thoughts, and drawings, and a plastic The Jetsons cup in a neat row. She inspects her grimoire, candles, hexagrams and other spell paraphernalia in the hearth. She lays down and jiggles her legs. Then she gets up, sifts through her clothes again and changes into a new outfit, slipping into a pair of light cotton black and grey checked pants and a small black t-shirt that says Chrome. The small t-shirt hangs loosely on her emaciated frame. She's had the pants since high school and is amazed that she hasn't lost them too. She decides to wrap a scarf tightly around her hips and layers her studded leather belt over that.

While she's inspecting her things and getting dressed, Babs yearns for her lost skateboard again. She pulls on an almost clean pair of socks that she handwashes in the kitchen sink- sometimes with soap, sometimes not. They dry stiffly and soften with wear. Then she dons a pair of soft leather booties that fold over at the ankle. Not great for skating, but since there's no board… She sighs.

Babs looks around. There is nothing else for her to do. She opens her small black daypack with the one busted shoulder strap, folds the newspaper in half, and stuffs that into the pack along with her new pen, notebook, and gum. She adds her ratty high-tops, culottes and some clean underwear: something to leave at Carla's, just in case.

She calls Luna softly once again, and after waiting a beat, straps Carla's leather purse across her chest, loops her pack over one arm, and tiptoes down the stairs and safely to freedom from Annie's prying eyes for now.

On a mission now, Babs walks over to Petrini's, gets change for a five, and sets up a little office at the phone mounted in front of the store. She calls every place she has circled and makes notes in her little pad with appointments for two places right here in the Haight, tomorrow, and two smaller apartments in the Castro, tomorrow and the day after that. This is fun! It's like a treasure hunt, with the apartment as the prize.

To kill time, Babs decides to check out the Haight apartments now. She can at least see what they look like from the outside and add those images to the pictures in her head. She walks up to McAllister past Stanyon and finds the first place on her list. It's a sort of box-shaped simple structure without all the filigree so prevalent on fancier houses around the City. There is an unmarked storefront downstairs with large sheets of brown paper across its wide, flat windows, and a single entrance to the side of that, leading upstairs. It looks like there might be only the one apartment and she likes that. No neighbors. And whatever the business is downstairs won't mind her all-night customers. This is the place, she decides, even though she hasn't been inside or filled anything out yet. Babs always makes quick decisions like this. Sometimes that's got her into trouble, but so far so good. Look at where she is now.

Babs can't wait any longer. Since this is the place she has decided to move into, there's nothing left for her to do in the Haight, so she might as well head over to Carla's now. She grabs the 5 down to Union Square, and the 8 up to Kearny. As she steps onto the street from the bus, she realizes she should have gone a few more blocks to Carla's. No matter. She likes looking in all the store windows between here and Carla's place. She meanders on her way to Grant Street and plays a little game while she walks. In each store window, she chooses one thing she would buy for herself. She brings out her notepad and pen and starts to make another list but quits after the eighth or ninth store. She can always come back and buy anything she wants some other time. No need for another list for now.

As she passes one store, she notes the time on a clock in the window. Dammit, it's only 5:30. She's so early. She hopes Carla is home, and awake, and doesn't get pissed off at her for coming over hours before the time they'd agreed upon. As Babs is standing there, trying to decide what to do, the door of the store she is standing in front of opens with a tinkle from the bell mounted over the door. Ooo thinks Babs. I should get one of those for my place. Then she looks up into Carla's wide-grinning face.

"Babs! What are you doing up here already?!" Carla turns to look at the clock in the window. You're not supposed to be here for another... three hours." She stands with her hands on her hips in mock disciplinary dismay. Babs starts to sputter, "Oh, sorry... I, um... didn't have any place else to go." She adds, "Annie broke into my room again, so I couldn't stay there..."

Carla holds up both hands, "Whoa... slow down. I'm kidding. I'm glad you're here, because actually, I have something for you." She grins again as she reaches into the pocket of her short denim shorts she's wearing over ripped fishnet stockings and ballet flats, everything in varying shades of white. She says, "Hold out your hand and close your eyes." Babs leans against the building, out of the way of people jostling past them on the sidewalk. She closes her eyes and holds out one hand. Carla drops something small, metal, ridged into the palm of her hand.

"I made you a key like we talked about earlier. I figure until you get your own place, you can't stash anything at Annie's. She won't like the competition. I know you don't fuck a lot of boys or have crazy parties, so..."

Babs throws her arms around Carla's shoulders and catches her in a brief, stiff hug. Carla doesn't even have time to hug her back. Babs purrs, "Thank you!! You have no idea..."

4

As they walk up the hill, Babs tells her Sister of Night Light everything she's accomplished since they separated earlier in the day. Apartment hunting, note-taking, decision making... "And a fresh buzz!" Carla swipes one hand lightly across Babs' shorn skull.

At the apartment, Carla stands aside so Babs can see if her new key works in the lock. It does. Carla hands her the second key as they stand at the top of the stairs so Babs has one each for both the front and apartment doors.

They decide to celebrate with a small bump. Babs smacks herself lightly on the forehead. She forgot to pack her kit. Carla doesn't mind sharing a needle with her but one of them will have to see about getting a fresh rig. Maybe Babs can find out where Shelly gets hers or find another source. That would be smart. It goes in the notepad.

They complete their ritual, and once Carla has put her works away and cleaned a corner of the kitchen counter, they settle in for smokes on the balcony. Babs shares more of her plans for her new place with Carla, who nods and offers suggestions for the décor. They chat about what Babs will do with two bedrooms. What to do with all that extra space? Babs lights a fresh cigarette and blows smoke rings towards the lock and chain on the railing. "So... you know what I was thinking? If it's ok with you, I'd like to leave everything... all this..." - she gestures to the lacquered box and her backpack- "at your place for now. Is that ok?" Carla leans over and nudges Babs with her shoulder. "Of course, silly-billy. That's what the key is for."

Babs decides then and there that Carla's place should be called the Sisterhood of Night Light-House, and her place can be the Bat Cave. That makes perfect sense. So much sense that she doesn't even need to write it down. The two hang out, smoking and yakking about Babs' plans, and about the photos Carla plans to take later tonight. At one point, they realize the streetlights outside have switched on. It's dark out, and oh shit! Time to head over to the Mab and get to work.

Babs doesn't even know who's playing tonight, just that there is a show, and where there is a show, there are punks. And where there are punks, there are punks who are looking for speed. Time to get a move on and see what she can do with all this product. She's never had so much to sell before and she's a little nervous about it. Carla is flustered that she missed her sunset hour at Coit, so she changes her plans and decides to join Babs at the club. Who knows, maybe Red will be there and they can catch up. Or even Gabe, though she's not sure what she wants to do about that.

Carla swipes warpath streaks across her cheeks in chrome green and yellow eyeshadow, and runs heavy black kohl around her eyes. She's ready. Babs checks the small leather purse to make sure she has enough product, cigs, lighter, keys. All set. Notepad and pen? They don't fit, so... she hates to leave them behind. She needs a bigger bag. That goes on the list, and out the door they fly.

The two walk briskly up Grant to Broadway and cross the street beneath Carol Doda's brightly lit boobs to the large two-tone building with its bright yellow sign advertising Filipino cuisine and cocktails. The sidewalk is packed with punks and 'normy' folks out for the night, milling and smoking and trying to make deals. Babs looks up at the other can attached to the building, the vertical white neon on black 'On Broadway' and realizes there might be two shows tonight.

Lately, more well-known names play upstairs at the bigger venue, which explains the unusual crowd. Those shows tend to cost more than the rattier local bands playing downstairs. Babs is friendly with the door guy Troy though, and he usually lets her go back and forth between the two venues. Hopefully he's there and will help her out tonight. Especially tonight. Babs looks up at Carla, takes a deep breath, and sidles into the lip of the crowd.

She looks back at Carla who is standing with one foot in the street and one foot on the sidewalk, undecided. She tells her pale friend, "I'm gonna see what's going on down here first, then I'll try to go upstairs. So I might be here or there." She waves one hand and threads through packed bodies to the Mab's open door.

She pushes her way through the crowded narrow hall to the back of the room where she hopes for a spot by the bathrooms. There, she can get her bearings and see who is in the room and looking for what she's selling. She bumps into and says 'Hey' to a bunch of punks she knows. Past the bar, the room is throbbing in cool chaos. The band on stage has the crowd whipping around and around in a sweaty frenzy. Babs doesn't like getting close to the pit, but tonight the whole room is seething, undulating, and rocking to the driving jungle beat of the drums and nearly falsetto bee-like buzz of the guitar.

Babs pushes through the crowd to the back of the venue. She's starting to feel claustrophobic already, and she's only been here a minute. She wishes she was taller, like Carla or Val and Sophie. Bodies press in against her from all sides and swallow her up, so she feels like the incredible shrinking woman from that old black and white movie. Get to the bathroom, Babs, she repeats to herself over and over.

Of course, the line to the women's restroom is more like a gaggle of punks pressing in towards its sweating, peeling door. Exiting punkettes have to fight their way out through the crowd. Babs starts to shove her way through more aggressively, pushing past the 'Hey!'s and 'Fuck YOU!'s barked out around her. The guitar plays a familiar string of notes- is that something Middle Eastern? How would she know that, she wonders. The drums gallop furiously and the band launches into a full-on sensory assault. The room erupts, becoming one giant pulsing and swaying organism. Arms and fists pump and flail as blurry punks are absorbed into the teeming mosh-blob.

Babs takes advantage of the bathroom crowd's distraction as a number of the punkettes around her sing along, "Tonight we're taking my fast car, we're gonna go down to the cowboy bar!" She pushes her way successfully to the door and squeezes herself inside. Too bad, she was starting to like this song, whoever they are. The flyers out front had said all the bands are from SoCal but Babs doesn't really bother herself with the names of most bands. She just knows the songs she likes, and her special faves of course, like Bauhaus, Bowie and Patti Smith.

Babs is pressed up against the door inside the impossibly small bathroom. She slides over to the wall in front of the two stalls and waits. She's almost there. She can feel the driving drums through the wall at her back and begins to tap a foot as the main room hollers, "I want! To be! A cowboy!" She cracks up. The punkette wedged against Babs glances at her with sharp black winged cats-eyes and black-stenciled lips. She chuckles too. "Yeah, right... I don't want to be a fucking cowboy..." Babs grins and turns her attention to the bathroom stall doors. Open, open, open, she thinks.

"Babs! Hi, honey!" Babs looks up at the refrigerator-sized woman easing her way past the stalls to the door. Her red 1950's hairdo is slightly askew and the heavy foundation she's wearing is creased down her neck. "Hey Mary," Babs smiles. Babs doesn't know if it's true, but what she's heard is that Mary used to be a college football player, and is now... well, Mary. She holds up the leather purse with both hands. "Are you looking for anything delish?" Mary claps her hands together and sings, "Oh hell yes!" Babs turns towards the wall and nods her head to suggest that Mary do so as well. Mary leans her large body against the wall, framing Babs in.

"You have dimes?" Babs snorts, of course. She opens the small purse, sorts through the sandwich bags that hold different sized portions, and selects a perfectly gorgeous pale green dime baggie. Mary gasps when she sees it. "What is that? It's so pretty...! It's ten, right?" Babs shakes her head no. "Sorry, I should have said. This is super stuff. Uncut rocks. And I'm the only one who has it!" She adds gleefully. Mary raises one eyebrow. "So, seventy-five a quarter, thirty a dime." Mary's eyes dim and her mouth turns down at the edges. "I can't afford that…"

Babs doesn't hesitate. She's always liked Mary, and besides, this is her first sale. She needs to get the word out about how amazing this shit is, which Babs knows Mary will do. "Ok, for you, twenty. Trust me, less goes farther with this. And there will be more." She smiles encouragingly, and Mary nods, ok. She digs around in her own purse, a burnt-orange 1970's handbag with large silver clasps, and hands Babs a rumpled twenty-dollar bill. Babs places the small glassine envelope into Mary's large hand, and grinds her teeth absentmindedly. First sale, if you don't count the big thing with Jenn. Mary pinches the edge of the envelope between two fingers and holds it up to the fluorescent light above her head. "Oooo… so pretty!"

A number of punkettes packed around them look up to see what she has in her hand. Some glance down at Babs. She holds up her leather purse and nods, yup. They lean in. One of the stall doors opens and Mary cuts inside ahead of the next punkette waiting to pee. "Hey!" The punkette tries to grab the edge of the metal door but Mary is stronger and pulls it closed. The punkette turns her head to make eye contact with everyone around her, "What the fuck?" The cats-eye punkette points at Babs, who is still holding up her purse. "Oh." She sighs. "Well, whatchya got?" Babs tilts her head to her left, urging the punkette to stand by her side. She steps in, and the Bat Cave is on.

In less than an hour, Babs is almost sold out. She's been mixing and matching prices according to what each punkette seems to be willing and able to pay. She began to call the dime bags quarters, which- even though they technically aren't- can get someone as high as any twenty-five-dollar powder bags out there. You break up these pretty little rocks, cut them up, and they do expand in size. So technically, she's not lying... She's been shoving crumpled bills into the pockets of her pants- there's not enough room in the tiny purse for the wadded-up bills and product, even though the carefully measured envelopes are dwindling fast.

Babs is thirsty and needs to get the fuck out of this cramped space. She doesn't feel claustrophobic anymore- that's usually reserved for thick crowds like out in the club. But she needs to see what's going on out there and step outside for a smoke and some air. She thinks she'll run back up to Carla's, re-up her supply, and come back to see what's happening upstairs too. The night is so young.

Babs slides through the bathroom door and eases herself against the wall between the men's and women's toilets. The band just stopped playing and the emcee has grabbed the microphone and is cussing out the crowd. The room isn't seething any more. Punks mill around, waiting for the next band to step onto the stage and play. As the emcee hurls insults at the room, punks shout back and spit on the stage. Some throw bottles or just pump their fists or middles fingers into the air. Cool, thinks Babs. She waves at Bags, standing near the bar, and Red, fully gussied up in his stiff leather and gleaming scalp.

As she weaves her way to the exit, Babs briefly wonders where Carla might be. Someone knocks into her sharply, jarring her gritted teeth, so she concentrates on getting outside. At the door, she thanks Troy and squeezes into the damp night. It's been raining. The street is wet, and punks are huddled together with upturned collars and shoulders hunched against the dank.

Babs pauses underneath the awning, wishing she still had her leather. That's one more thing Annie has taken off her hands in exchange for rent. She mutters, "Fuck," and walks over to the edge of a sodden punk circle where she pulls out a cigarette and tries to keep it dry as she lights it. Making sure the purse is firmly closed, Babs looks both ways before she crosses the shiny street. She sings "I want. To be. A cowboy," to herself over and over in time to her quick footsteps back up the hill.

At the apartment, Babs drops her bag inside the door, grabs a towel from the bathroom to dry off, and stands in the main room, looking around. Does Carla have a jacket she can borrow? A hat? She needs a bigger purse or something to carry this next batch of product back up to Broadway. Not her broken-down backpack. She approaches the Murphy bed- still put away- and begins opening and closing drawers, looking for something to wear and something to carry the speed in. She knows she should feel guilty about poking around, but Carla gave her the keys to her place. Babs is sure this is fine.

There are some underthings, plastic sleeves of negatives, and cannisters of film. One drawer is full of letters and a shoebox crammed with postcards and translucent paper Tibetan things. Interesting, but nothing she needs. Then Babs notices a narrow door off to one side of the Murphy bed. Cool, a closet. Opening it, she fingers a mohair sweater, some more of those white underwear gowns, and behind everything else, there's a tan light wool raincoat. Perfect. It's not cold outside, but if she leaves it open and just turns up the collar, she should be fine. And dry. There are two pairs of shoes crammed in at the front of the tiny closet. Babs pushes the dresses aside to see what might be behind them, and eureka! There's a larger version of the purse she's been carrying resting against the back wall. She grabs that and the coat and drops them in the middle of the floor. Shopping at Carla's is fun. Squatting, Babs empties the few remaining quarters from the first purse onto the floor. She pulls wads of cash out of her pockets and jumps up to grab the lacquer box from the balcony room.

Babs plonks herself down in the middle of all this booty and takes a deep breath to slow down. She touches some of the money tentatively. Holy shit, that's a lot of moolah. She starts counting and stacking the bills so they all face the same direction, and stops counting as she separates ones from fives, tens and twenties. Once they're all stacked neatly, and more or less smoothed out, Babs counts the cash into piles of one hundred dollars, lining them up side by side. She counts it all again and makes little scratch marks in her notebook: four little lines with one line across equals five hundred dollars. As she counts and scribbles, she places those five-hundred-dollar bundles off to the side. She tucks the remaining ones and fives up against her ankle beneath her sock, counts the scratch marks, and counts them again.

"Oh my God." Babs shakes her head in disbelief as a smile unfurls across her face. There is almost sixty-five hundred dollars here. Enough to get her place already or put aside to buy more product, sell more, then get the place. This is unreal. Is she so high, she's counting wrong? Maybe she's hallucinating a little? Uh... She collects the money carefully and very slowly and methodically counts it all once again.

Sure enough, sixty-four hundred bucks, and whatever's in her sock. She picks up her notebook and finds a fresh page, then pauses, trying to think what to write. From her budget, if she had sold each gram as she'd planned, she should have eighty-four hundred dollars. Her shoulders tense as she realizes the cost of her uncertainty back at the club. She needs to firm up her prices, or maybe sell smaller amounts for more, like she was selling the dime bags as quarters. She decides that's best, counts out twenty-five quarter bag cellophane envelopes, and takes them to the kitchen where her scale awaits her. She opens each bag, carefully breaks them down into smaller denominations, seals the newly weighed envelopes and writes a five or ten on their price tags. She re-uses all the old envelopes: waste not, want not.

Babs puts the weights away and carries seventy-five fresh bags back into the main front room. There, she places nickel bags (priced at ten bucks) in one sandwich baggie, dime bags (priced at twenty) in another. She puts twenty quarter bags ('seventy dollars!' she affirms, since these haven't been re-weighed out) in a larger baggie and tucks them all, side by side, in the belly of the larger leather purse.

She ponders a moment and tears out her old budget calculations from the notebook. Turning to a fresh page, she writes out new calculations, including the discounts she'd already let slip. Satisfied, Babs tucks the notebook, pen, cigs and lighter into the purse's pocket. She stuffs all that cash into a paper envelope and places it on top of her remaining stock inside the lacquer box. She wishes she had someplace else to put the money. She's worried it will taint the pristine, pretty little rocks. Then she looks up. Oh, her crappy backpack! She grabs the envelope, rushes over to the balcony room where her backpack rests against a wall, and shoves the envelope to the bottom beneath her panties and things.

Babs rolls her shoulders. They always seize up when she gets high and then concentrates on a project. Whether she's making notes, hunched over doodling, building something from trash, or casting a spell, her shoulders clench up, her lower back pinches, even the arches of her feet get cramps. Nothing a little stretch and a hot shower won't cure. Maybe some sleep too, but not now.

Babs looks around the tiny apartment. It's nice of Carla to give me the keys, she thinks again, but I need to get a place pronto. It just feels... intrusive. And Carla's place is so neat, everything put away and so clean. Babs looks at her backpack and down at what she's wearing. Everything she owns is black, and everything Carla likes is white. She feels like she needs to hide her stuff. Not just in the small balcony room, but... she glances at the white-washed trunk with its row of candles across the top. No... She turns and looks at the kitchen doorway. Someplace in there? That's doesn't seem right either. Then Babs thinks, 'of course'. She picks up the smaller leather purse, her backpack and the lacquered box, and stacks them as neatly as she can at the back of Carla's closet. She looks around the room. It's like she's not even here. Perfect.

Checking the contents once again of the larger purse, Babs decides she's ready. She took longer than she thought she would, but she's pretty sure there should be plenty going on either at the Mab or upstairs at OB. She picks up Carla's tan raincoat, steps onto the landing and pulls the door shut, making sure to listen for the click of the lock tumbling into place. Then she shrugs on the coat as she trips down the stairs onto Grant and into the night once more.

5

It's stopped drizzling and now there is a fog-like mist hovering about the street. Babs wraps the raincoat around her body and starts trotting back to the club. Her footsteps echo slightly tap tap tap, reminding her of a song, but she can't remember how it goes or who it's by.

There are new groups of punks gathered together on the sidewalk outside the club. Babs contemplates the entrance and decides to check out what's happening upstairs. Tony is still at the door, and he waves her on up. He knows what she's up to. Maybe she'll give him a taste.

She climbs the narrow staircase that lands her in a thicket of bodies. They smell like sweat, cigarettes, stale beer, and patchouli. Her chest tightens and she struggles to catch her breath. Babs shoves her way past bodies and more bodies, not even checking to see who she might know in the crowd. A deep, distorted wah wah wah pulses through the walled-in insulation of punks around her. She desperately needs to get to the balcony where she can get the lay of the room and maybe set up shop. She makes her way upstairs where there are still a lot of punks, but more room, and Babs' chest relaxes. She peels off the raincoat, wishing she hadn't borrowed it after all. It's going to stink like the club, but hopefully it won't be so bad.

At the end of the balcony nearest the stage, punks are pressed together in a cluster, leaning out dangerously over the railing, absorbed in the band below. Furthest from the stage, where Babs passes couples sucking face and rocking to the grinding noise of the band and the singer's taunting banter, there is more space. She starts to look around to see who she knows. She recognizes a few punks from around town, the soup kitchen and the Haight. She makes eye contact when she can, lifts her bag to show she's carrying, and leans over a free spot at the balcony.

"Yes I know... Now I know..." speak-sings the singer. He's naked from the waist up, his pale chest glistening in the harsh stage lights. His dirty black jeans ride low on his hips as he grasps the microphone in one sweaty hand and holds the mic cable in the other. He leans out over the crowd, seeming to mock them as he dances from one end of the stage and back. Someone lifts a blonde girl sporting an I Dream of Jeannie ponytail onto the stage where she tries to twirl around and around the lead singer. He keeps singing, pretends to dance with her, then ignores her and leans back out over the seething crowd. She pouts and disappears offstage. A punk jumps up next to the singer, staggers a few steps, and launches himself into the crowd, followed by one punk after the other. They each stumble up onto the stage, take a few steps, and catapult themselves back into the pit. Babs thinks they look like one of those Swiss clocks where a little man pops out here and goes back in there.

Two guitars and electric bass dig in, loudly distorted and synchronized behind the dancing, taunting speak-shout-singer. Droplets of his sweat fly out over the punks crowded against the edge of the stage. Babs is fascinated by the show and doesn't notice when a couple of punkettes line up behind her. One of them taps her on the shoulder. "Babs?" She turns and thinks, 'Bat Cave start your engines'. She shifts the raincoat from one arm to the other, and says, "Hey. Let's go out on the balcony."

Babs and the two punkettes weave their way out to the narrow balcony. There are no tables, so they wedge themselves against the wall, form a barrier with their bodies, and Babs makes a sale. When the punkettes leave, another takes their spot. And so it goes. Babs sees faces she knows, says 'hey' or chats with them a bit. The music thuds through the wall at Babs' shoulder. She sells more speed. She's thirsty again but doesn't want to give up this prime spot. Punks looking for meth know where to find her by now, but she's not too exposed. She begins to wonder if she should do another bump or stay here in her temporary office until she sells out. She licks her lips and decides to stay. She's starting to feel a little ragged, even though she slept the night before. A lot has happened today, so maybe more sleep isn't a bad idea.

Oh! And she needs to be in the Haight early tomorrow to see the place she already thinks of as hers. So, she needs to finish up here, drop everything at Carla's, and head back to the squat. She might not get much sleep, but at least she'll be in the Haight for her morning appointment.

There is a brief lag between buyers for a minute, so Babs checks the contents of her purse. Only two dimes and three quarters left. The music has stopped playing but punks coming out to the balcony aren't looking for her. She wonders if she should be logging any of this in her notebook, then decides she needs a book with tabs so she can keep track of the different strings of thought bouncing around her brain: selling product, the apartment and all it will require, stuff she wants generally, plans for a trip to New York? Los Angeles? London?

Babs recognizes one of the punks who just stepped outside-Suburban's girlfriend Mimi. Her eyes are heavily rimmed in kohl, and she wears her peroxided blond hair radiating in long spikes every which way. "Hey MimI, is the show done for the night?" Just then, they hear from inside, "Eat! It!" And another band- or is it the same band? It sounds the same to Babs- starts crashing and grinding and shout-singing again. "Never mind," Babs grinds her teeth. Woo, she's coming down. Should she do a line or go back to Haight? She decides to head inside, walk the perimeter if it's not too crowded, pass through the Mab, and try to find Carla. Then she can drop funds and get over to the Haight. That's a good plan.

She starts to go back inside, but Mimi stops her. "Hey, I hear you have some awesome little moon rocks. Do you still...?" Babs leans back against the wall, "Yup. Whatchya need?" She's amazed she never tried anything like this before. She's usually been good for a nickel or dime at shows. She would nearly support her own habit by buying a gram, breaking it up, using what she wants, and selling the rest so she can buy more. Sometimes- most of the time- she uses more than she plans to, leaving her with less to sell and no funds to re-up. But this... there's enough for her to enjoy a taste, sell to buy more, and buy stuff she needs. Her mind is spinning from how different things are from only a few days ago. She hopes again that she isn't hallucinating. She's pretty sure she's at the OB and Mab, making big sales, and about to get an apartment away from the squat where she's felt like a prisoner for some time.

Babs shows Mimi her wares, Mimi chooses, and they head back inside where they part ways- Mimi to the bathroom to do a shot, Babs walking the balcony to finish up. She runs across a few more punks she knows but no-one interested in her goods. As she heads downstairs, one punkette stops her and buys for the second time that night, cool. Babs looks at the throbbing crowd and decides she's done. She's been sucked into mosh chaos before no matter how much she clings to the walls. She slinks over to the staircase and looks around one last time while nodding to the compelling grind of the band- whoever they are- and their lead singer shout-singing to the crowd. She wishes she knew their name. She wouldn't mind seeing them again, but right now she feels like she's coming down harder, so it's time to finish up and call it a night.

Babs presses her way down the stairs almost blindly, avoiding eye contact and punks she knows. Downstairs, she says 'Gnight' to some other guy at the door, and crosses over to the entrance to The Mab. Inside, as she passes the bar and bathrooms on her way to the main floor, some punk she doesn't recognize stops her and asks, "Hey you're that git selling moon rocks, arenchya?" Babs cracks a smile. Moon rocks it is then.

"Sure, whatchya need?"

The punk licks his lips. He's cute, she thinks, looking over his short, red-dyed hair, flinty blue eyes, sharp cheekbones, and wiry, narrow-hipped frame. She puts some serious flirt into her smile, though he's probably not paying attention. He wants one thing, and she's selling him that. Deal done, Babs introduces herself. He says, "Alright see you around," tips one of his hands in a small salute and walks off. So much for flirting, she sighs.

From where she stands, Babs can see just the back and outline of the crowd. They're still moshing, though much slower than before. She sees Red at the Bar again. He raises a hand in greeting, and she waves back. Must be a good show for Red to stick around this long. Babs goes over and stands on tiptoe to yell into his ear. "Have you seen Carla?"

"What?!" He yells back. Babs leans back and yells in his direction, "...Carla?!"

"Oh, yeah! She's..." he jerks his thumb towards the exit. She's either outside or she went home. Babs raises her thumb in thanks, scans the room, and decides, 'Yup, I'm toast.' She touches Red on the shoulder, waves her hand in front of his face 'Bye', and scoots out the exit once more.

Outside, some punk she knows from Fulton House– she can't remember his name- pulls her aside and asks what she's got. Word is spreading. Pretty soon, once she has her place, she won't need to make the rounds at show like this unless she wants to go the show. Pretty soon, but for now, they walk to the end of the building and its narrow alleyway, tuck themselves around the corner, and make a deal.

Sliding her arms into Carla's raincoat, Babs stands at the precipice between punks exiting the building in couples and small groups and the empty street to her left. Her body feels heavy. She starts up Broadway towards Grant and the pale sanctuary of Carla's apartment, singing "I want. To be. A cowboy..."

She walks faster. She's not carrying as much product and money as before, but she's not as high, so she's suddenly scared of being rolled or worse. She thinks about this training thing she's going to do with Ed next week and wishes it was sooner, or already done. Even if she doesn't come out to shows packing product anymore, she believes she will feel safer after Ed shows her stuff. He hasn't steered her wrong yet, though she hasn't known him that long.

Walking up Grant, Babs stiffens as a lone male figure crosses the street and approaches her. The streetlight is behind him, so she can't make out who it is. He's walking with a hitch, shoulders hunched inside his leather jacket; hands stuffed deep into the front pockets of his jeans. The streetlight makes a halo of his short spiked blond hair. So many punks have been bleaching their hair lately. Babs likes to dye hers wild colors instead. As he closes in, she sees who it is and relaxes. It's Pat's son, Paulie. He's harmless, unless you count all the punkettes he's given herpes to.

"Hey Paulie." Babs turns her shoulder so they can pass each other without touching. He holds out one hand. "Hey! No! I was trying to find you. I hear you're dealing now."

Babs looks back down the sidewalk towards the club. She turns back to Paulie. "Yeah..." He grimaces thinly. "Do you have... is it just speed? Or are you also selling H?" Of course, she knows the desperate emptiness in his eyes. He's jonesing hard and needs a hit, just not what she's selling.

"No, sorry Paulie. Have you tried Shelly? Or Marco? I don't know, Jenn? I don't really know that scene..."

He scowls and wipes one hand through his greasy hair. "Yeah, no..." He shoves his hands back into his pockets and presses his arms tightly to his sides. "I can't..." Ah, right. Babs has heard the stories. Paulie has borrowed and promised and ripped off most everyone in the heroin community. He probably can't go to any of those dealers, since he most likely owes most of them money, favors and apologies he can't spare. She shrugs her shoulders and steps around him, "Sorry…"

Paulie reaches out and grabs her arm. "Can I come to your place?" He looks up the street. "Where you going anyway?" He tries to smile again but it comes across as hungry and greedy. "I'm going to a private thing, sorry." She shrugs off his arm and takes a step back.

"Please…? I'll be so quiet. You won't know I'm there." Fuck, he's like glue. Paulie is so hard to shake off when he gloms on, once he's decided you have what he wants. She takes another step back. "No, sorry. It really is a private thing." She decides to lie. "It's a guy, ok? I'm going to meet someone. We're going to fuck, ok?!"

Paulie's shoulders slump. "Oh…" Babs locks her knees and tries to stand taller. Paulie has been known to do crazy things. Once he followed an ex-girlfriend on his knees for blocks through Union Square where she worked. She told everyone how pitiful he was, crying and holding out his arms like he wanted her stop and pick him up. Another ex-girlfriend spread the story about Paulie visiting her after she moved away from San Francisco, saying he missed her so much. But he'd shown up with a wife, both desperate to score, all the way from the other side of the State.

So Babs is standing her ground. There's no knowing what he might do. She heard he's even carrying a knife these days that he's pulled on a few punks. No way is she going to let that happen to her. She takes a few more measured steps back. "Ok, I gotta go." She points down Grant towards the Mab. "There's plenty of people at both shows. Try there?"

Paulie whimpers and looks pathetic. 'Fucking get a life', she thinks. "I really gotta go. Bye Paulie." She waits until he starts limping his way down the street. Once he reaches the corner, she turns and sprints up Grant to Carla's. A few doors up, she stops and looks back. He's gone. She lets herself in through Carla's front door and takes the stairs two at a time, as lightly as she can, though fuck the landlady.

At the top of the stairwell, Babs puts the other key in the lock, but the door swings open. Carla is freshly showered and dressed in socks and a man's long button-down striped shirt. Sorta brat pack, Babs thinks to herself. She likes it. "Sssssshhhhhh..." Carla has one finger pressed against her lips. She waves Babs inside. "So, how'd it go tonight?" She frowns. "Hey, is that my Burberry?"

Babs looks down at the raincoat she is wearing. "Uh, yeah, is that what this is called?" She chews her lower lip. "It was raining, and I came back to drop off money and get more stuff. I didn't want to get wet on the way back, so I borrowed it." She looks at Carla, worried she fucked up. "Is that ok? Sorry... I went through your closet to find a bigger bag to carry stuff in." Carla waves both hands in the air, "Psshhh. That's fine. It's not even wet." She leans in to sniff. "But it does smell. Let me hang it out before putting it away."

Babs shrugs off the coat and hands it to Carla, who takes it into the kitchen where she opens a small back door that Babs didn't know existed. Carla does something with the coat, shuts the door, and comes back into the main room. The Murphy bed is down, all made up with clean white sheets and a Delft blue comforter. Wow, just like in some kind of fancy magazine, thinks Babs.

She sits on the floor and starts organizing bills like before-face up in one direction, in one-hundred-dollar stacks. She grabs her notebook and pen, counts out the piles, and makes further notes on the accounting page. Grinning, she looks at Carla, who has perched quietly on the end of the bed, watching and waiting for Babs to finish.

Babs shakes her head in disbelief, yet it's believable, because the money is right there. "That's another three thousand," she stacks the bills in order of denomination and shows Carla. "I put that box you gave me in your closet so it's not just sitting out with all this cash," she explains. She stands to open the closet, then pauses and looks at Carla. "Can I...?" Carla has lain back on the bed, arms extended over her head. She wiggles her fingers. "Sure, sure."

As Babs opens the closet and pulls out the lacquered box, she says, "I put the purse you lent me back. See? I'll give this bigger one back as soon as I get something else." She holds up the smaller purse to show where it is. Carla turns over on her side to look. Babs adds, "I'm heading back to Annie's tonight, since I need to be in the Haight to look at apartments tomorrow. Might as well stay the night there." She mixes the new bills in with the other money- ones with ones, fives with fives, and so on. "Is it ok if I leave this here until I get my place? I'll try not to take up your space much longer."

Carla rolls over onto her back again. "I don't mind you leaving stuff here. Babs, that's why I gave you the keys. And for a bag? Go to that Tibetan hippie place on Haight near the Red Vic. They have pretty cool stuff you might like." She gazes at the ceiling.

Babs murmurs thanks, puts everything back in the closet and shuts the door. She still has the few bucks wedged in between her sock and boot, a dime she held onto, plus her cigs, bubble gum, notebook and pen. She is good to go. She brushes the creases out of her pants. "Ok, I'm gonna let you crash. I need to sleep too, somehow…" She grins and looks over at her friend. Carla's eyes are fluttering. She looks like a painting, posed like that, all stretched out along the clean blue and white bed. 'She's asleep!' she thinks and tiptoes out the door.

6

Out on the street, Babs tries to shake off the heavy feeling that's draped across her shoulders, cascading down her back. Yeah, she's coming down hard now. She needs to get back to Annie's and crash for a while. She wishes she had an alarm clock so she could be sure to wake up in time for her first appointment. Maybe Annie will have one she can borrow. Hopefully she won't try to charge her for it.

Babs walks up to Columbus and waits for the 91, which miraculously arrives in a few minutes. She takes it to Market where she switches to the 5 headed to Ocean Beach. As she leans her head against the window, she wishes she could get a place out near the beach. She could skate back and forth to the Haight, get that skate thing a bunch of punks used to do every Sunday going again. But that's not smart. That would be too far for buyers to travel to score. She would have to do her business at shows all the time, just like tonight. And even Babs knows that's not safe, as new as she is at this level of things. She closes her eyes and presses her forehead into the window.

What feels like only a moment later, she snaps her eyes open in the glare of the bus's interior lights and looks around, confused. Where is she? She tries to focus but can't figure out what's going on until the bus comes to a full stop.

Oh, they're at Lyon and McAllister. Couple more stops and she can walk the rest of the way. Babs squares her shoulders and runs one hand through her hair. 'Wake up,' she tells herself. That's stupid, falling asleep on the bus. It's a good thing I wasn't driving, hah.

At her stop, she disembarks, walks the few blocks to the squat, and tries to make her way upstairs as quietly as possible. Who knows who or what Annie X is doing this time of night. A few steps creak, as they always do, and Babs bangs heavily into the door frame at the top of the landing. "Shit!" Annie is sitting in one of her lounging chairs, lighter in one hand, with a pile of paraphernalia laid out on the dainty table at her side. She laughs. "Hey stranger." She gestures to the other chair. She seems like she's in a good mood. Be careful...

Babs says, "Just a sec," and goes to her room to take off her boots, socks, and the leather bag. She puts the few dollars from her boot on the TV tray, squats to smell her feet- they're ok- and walks back into the other room. "What's going on? I haven't seen you in days." She sits in the other armchair and glances at what Annie has spread out on the little side table. There's a piece of aluminum foil, a glass tube, and a small wooden box with a glassine envelope of some brown and flecked white powder lying propped open inside it. Annie is smoking H, huh.

Annie picks up the creased aluminum. "You want?" Babs thinks, why not, and says, "Sure." Annie pours a little pyramid of the flecked powder onto one end of the sheet, hands Babs the glass tube, and holds the lighter out. "Say when." Babs places the glass tube between her lips, and mumbles 'when' around the glass. Annie flicks the lighter on. As the powder heats up, it melts and burbles, dribbling down the creased ravine. "Get it!" Annie says. Babs inhales, chasing the drip and curl of smoke along the trench. She sucks it all in, tasting that dirty, mushroomy thing at the back of her throat. Immediately she feels her eyes roll up and smoky residue coats her teeth. "Gnnnhhhh..." The room swims out of focus. It feels like everything is swirling around and around. She knows it will stop, so she tries to relax into the high, low, whatever you call it. She hands the aluminum sheet in the general direction where Annie is sitting, sits back and closes her eyes. Mmmmmmmm... Just what the doctor ordered.

Annie chases her own dragon. Babs can hear the hiss of the flame and the sound of Annie inhaling. The faint scent of burning tar hangs in the air between them. They both sit in silence, though Babs wishes there was music. Bauhaus, something melodic she can ride like these waves crashing around her head.

"Cool... thanks Annie. Mm, hey, just so you know. I'm

looking at places tomorrow. Today. Don't know when, but I'm definitely getting out of your space soon, kay?" She tries to open her eyes, but it's so much easier to keep them shut. She lifts one hand and lets it drop again to the arm of the chair. Whew. It's been forever since Babs has done any heroin. Smoke or shoot. Damn. She can't even think what her next move should be. So she sits still.

Annie speaks so softly Babs almost misses it. "Alright. I was going to ask you about that. S'alright..." Babs eventually says, "Kay, I'm gonna go crash. Thanks for sharing..." She pushes herself up from the chair with effort, waves one hand at Annie in a half salute, and holding onto the wall, the door frame, the wall again, she makes her way to the back of the squat. Talk about feeling heavy... Now Babs' whole body feels weighted down by enormous hands gently pressing her down, down, down...

In her room, she kneels on the spare mattress, removes all her belts, and lays down with her face turned to one side. Whew. There is nothing in her head, just these waves going 'pshhh... pshhh...' She half wonders if she should get undressed, but the thought evaporates before she can finish it. She hears a small scrnch scrnch scrnch and dreams someone is slicing into a turkey. Scrnch scrnch scrnch. Babs reaches one hand to her face to scratch her nose and lands on something soft and furry. A weight drops at the back of her throat, and she opens both eyes with all her willpower. What the fuh…? It's Luna, hunched over Babs' face, nibbling at the bridge of her nose.

Babs sits up, and the rat falls aside and scurries past her around the mattress and out the door. Babs touches the bridge of her nose. It's wet. She holds her fingers up. There is blood. Her fucking pet rat was just grazing on her nose, and now it's bleeding. She wants to go look at herself in the bathroom mirror but doesn't have the strength to get up. She's so tanked from coming down off all that speed and now she's high-low on H. Fuckit, it can't be that bad. She doesn't feel blood trickling down her face.

Babs grabs her scarf and dabs at her nose. She looks, and satisfied there isn't a ton of blood, she lays back down and drifts off into a cloud, dreaming of fairy tale characters and waves at the beach.

The number of foggy days over the city is never reported, reportedly. But take it from me—there's enough to satisfy everyone, and dissatisfy somebody."
— **Herb Caen, Don't Call It Frisco**

Do It Til You're Satisfied

1

Val shivers as she walks down Hayes. She glances up at second floor windows, looking for a clue. She's been to Marco's apartment before but forgot to write down the address before leaving Pat's, so she keeps walking, stopping to look, and walking on. It's a crisp, clear, very cold Thursday morning. She knows it's Thursday since this morning, their street crew driver reminded them that tomorrow is pay day. That's good, because she's down to her last dollar and rent is due next week. She can always panhandle- she's not shy about that- but that can be hit or miss.

Sometimes, you get generous drops in the hat. Sometimes de rien. She figures after she learns whatever Marco plans to teach her, she can panhandle down here. This end of the Haight usually has good pickings, so she can hopefully rake in enough to buy some beer and whatever stuff Marco says she'll need.

She rubs her hands up and down the arms of her raggedy mohair sweater. It's her fave, and even though it's unraveling, she still thinks it's the nicest thing she owns. She admires its deep blue and green jewel-toned squares and rubs her arms again, trying to build up a little heat. At the corner of Hayes and Webster, she stops. That's it. There's Marco's place. The classic Victorian is painted pale green with ornate cream trim, offset by olive rectangles beneath the eaves and each window.

Inside, instead of ratty second-hand furniture falling apart at the seams and greasy to the touch, Marco has a penchant for antiques and rich Oriental rugs. Val sees a few pieces in her mind: a satiny mauve floral brocade couch, a forest green loveseat with complex filigreed woodwork along the armrests, and some kind of odd loopy chair that faces two directions at once. You can sit in one seat, and he can sit in the other so that you are facing each other, side by side. Val thinks he calls that a love chair though she's not sure. Maybe that's just what she wants to call it. His apartment is filled with heavy, dark armoires and knick-knack shelves covered in fancy woodwork and spindly legs. She heard somewhere that he has someone come in and clean for him once a week. A punk having someone clean their apartment. That's just nuts.

Then again, Marco isn't just some punk. He moved to San

Francisco from Los Angeles a few years ago, and immediately cultivated this lifestyle, or maybe he was that way before. He started dealing heroin early on, and as long as she's known him, he's had this pseudo-Edwardian itch. You always see him in his Cuban boots, pressed trousers, high-collared shirts and frock coats, and when it's really cold, a heavy black woolen cape. Marco never goes to shows and doesn't hang at any of the squalid flea-ridden squats where most of the punks tend to live. He haunts used bookstores and deep dives into sorcery, surrounding himself with all that paraphernalia.

Val doesn't know anything about witchcraft, only that there are people around the punk scene who are very into it. She admires some of their totemic jewelry. That Babs wears a belt covered with tiny silver Milagros- hands, a human leg, crosses, birds, and hearts. Marco sports a thick leather bracelet embedded with a single human-looking green eye that stares at you. It watches you, unblinking, from all angles. Brrrr.... She shivers again.

Val presses the buzzer and waits for Marco to reply. They speak their 'who is it, it's me, come on up', and Marco buzzes her in. Val clomps up the flight of stairs to his second floor apartment, and is happily greeted by a rush of warm air. Her fingers and toes start to tingle immediately. "Damn! It's cold outside!"

Marco reaches out for a hug. He's a hugger, and it's never weird. "Val... long time no see. How are you?" He leads the way into his parlor and gestures towards her favorite loveseat. "Sit. Can I get you some tea?"

Val looks at Marco with an appraising eye. He looks good. Really good. The last time she saw him, he'd been frighteningly underweight. His black-dyed hair had been scraggly and greasy, hanging in clumps like palm tree fronds over his face, which was grey and pocked with faintly oozing scabs. He'd walked with a slight limp, both shoulders hunched as though trying to fold into himself.

But this Marco is a revelation of change. He stands as tall as his moderate height and slight frame allow. He's still limping a little, but his skin is clear, his lips are moist and full, and his eyes sparkle. Even his hair looks healthier. It's slicked back with a tapered tail at his neck. "Wow, Marco, you look great." She sits and unwinds her Kelly-Belly sewn burlap purse from the unraveling sleeve of her sweater and drops that on the floor. "I'm doing alright." She scratches to one side of her crotch. "Still doing trash pick-up for the City. Hanging with the Clits. We're doing an Outer Sunset run this weekend, I can hardly wait."

Marco holds out both hands, "Tea...?" Val smiles, "Oh, oui, merci." She leans back into the brocade cushion and waits as he putters in the other room. He's back momentarily- he must have had the tea kettle on- carrying a silver tray on which rests a pale pink teapot covered in small white blooms, and mis-matched teacups all adorned with varying pink flowers. Nestled between all the pretty colors, there's a small silver bowl filled with huge brown sugar cubes and a dainty white porcelain creamer shaped like a bird.

Val sits up, "Fancy!" Marco places the tray on the low, dark green table with its gold-embossed curved legs that sits neatly between the couches. He kneels on a green velvet pillow opposite Val and begins to serve. Val waits and observes. Marco has always been somewhat formal, but this tea thing is new. She wonders if it's part of his new health food thing he's doing. She makes a note to check out tea at Petrini's next time she has money for food.

Marco pours the tea into each cup through a small metal strainer- 'Chouette!' thinks Val. "Sugar? Milk? Or do you like lemon? Sorry, I don't have any, but I do have lemon juice." Val thinks, of course he does. There's something you do with lemon when you shoot heroin. She's never been interested in that sort of thing, so she's never really paid attention. "Sugar and milk are fine. Um... I thought you stopped... doing... heroin?"

Marco adds a misshapen lump of sugar and a dollop of milk

to her cup, places it on a saucer and hands it to her. "I did. But I keep it around for customers." He pours a little milk into his cup and sets the saucer down.

"Oh. I didn't know you were still dealing. I thought... with this health stuff you are doing, you stopped."

Marco smiles through closed lips. "That's my income. That's what I do. But I am eating a healthier diet. I mean, I still shoot smack once a month or so, just to test the stuff out. Mostly, I'm smoking hash these days, which is mind-altering. And I meditate. I even walk over to the Alamo to watch the sunrise some mornings." His lips split into a full toothsome smile.

Val nods in agreement. "Mon Dieu... whatever you're doing, you look fantastique." She takes a sip of her tea. It's creamy and sweet, with a faint bitter woodsy taste just like her grandma used to make. Just tea. She can do that. She clears her throat. "So, that's why I'm here. You told me you were starting to do healthy stuff, and lately, I've been feeling... not so great. En fait, I went to the clinic last week, and they tried to give me one of those 12 step pamphlet things. I'm not into any of that God bullsheet, but I thought I'd talk to you about what you said. I know I need to take better care of myself, but I don't want to quit doing speed. I just really want to know more about this health food stuff." She pauses and sips her tea again. "So I can get healthy too."

Marco shifts to sit cross-legged on the pillow. He takes a sip of his own tea. "That's good to hear. The food I buy isn't cheap though..." He stands. "Come here, let me show you." He takes a step towards the next room. Val carries her teacup and follows him into the bright, airy kitchen. Even that is like a picture in a magazine. Everything is so clean and sunny. She sniffs, not a whiff of trash anywhere. Marco opens the fridge and starts pointing at various things. "That's locally made yoghurt. That's organic milk. Those are all organic veggies and fruits." He shuts the fridge door and walks over to the cabinets mounted to each side of the sink. He opens one and shows her the boxes and sacks of things there. "Organic brown rice, black rice, lentils..." He shuts the cabinet and leans against the counter, facing Val. "I've been reading about what we put into our bodies- all the chemicals and preservatives they put into most foods- like chips, sugary cereals, even most kinds of bread. That can kill you faster than any drugs we put into our veins."

Val nods. She's not sure where she can find organic vegetables and fruit, or brown rice and all that sort of thing. "How cheap is not cheap? I see things that seem ok to me: rice, legumes, lettuce, apples, milk..."

Marco opens the fridge again and pulls out a carton of chocolate milk. "This is my one concession to 'not so healthy'. You figure, 'chocolate milk', cheap, right? Nope, this costs five bucks." Val snorts. She won't be buying that. "It's from a local dairy, and it's all organic. You can get regular milk from them too, but that costs almost as much." He puts the milk back in the fridge door and closes it. "Let's go sit down."

In the parlor, he pauses at the front bay window and lifts the shade to point at the small corner market across the street. "That place turned into a health food market about three months ago. At first, I stopped buying anything there. I was living off of cigarettes and pop-tarts, if you can call that living." He lets the shade drop. Val's mouth waters at the thought of a brown sugar pop-tart. They return to the couch and Marco sits cross-legged again on his pillow.

"Then I walked in one day while I was pretty high, and I don't know. I started checking out the labels. And they have some books and stuff up front. I bought a book called Whole Food Cooking. Most of it was boring at first, but then I started comparing some of what the book says with some of Crowley's writings and these Buddhist texts I've been reading, and something clicked. I went back over there," he waves a hand at the window, "and bought some rice and beans, some salad stuff, yoghurt... After a few failed experiments- I'm not a very good cook," he laughs. "I started feeling better. I don't really cook cook. I make salads and eat muesli and yoghurt. Lots of fruit and veggies.

Plain brown or black rice with veggies." He reaches over and touches a bruise on Val's thin forearm. "I stopped getting sores on my arms, and bruises. And my teeth stopped feeling all loose and wobbly." He circles Val's bruise with one finger then removes his hand.

Val is trying to keep up. "But those don't seem like they should be expensive things. Rice, beans, vegetables, milk... I love yoghurt. I used to eat this all the time as a child."

Marco pours them each some more tea. "Yeah, those are simple things. But if you buy organic, it costs more. And organic is the way you avoid all those chemicals."

"Ok, organic. Is this the only place to get this?" She waves to the window. "I don't think Petrini's or Safeway has this." Marco shakes his head. "Nope, there are other health food stores. There's that one little grocery up on Haight by you- that hippie place. I doubt if Safeway or Petrini's carries anything organic."

He blows on his tea. "If you want to try this out, I can lend you that book and give you some basics- beans, rice, yoghurt, muesli- to get started. But you'll have to do the rest. Cook it, eat it, keep at it. Val, you look like shit, I gotta say."

She turns her mouth down in a mock pout, but she knows he's right. She's way too thin, her skin is waxy, and she's always cold, even when the sun is shining. She can't catch her breath after only a block of skating, and worst of all, she can't paint if she's not high. It's like her imagination is sick too. She thinks maybe doing what Marco has been doing will fix things. If she can feel better and still keep shooting speed for fun, that would be perfect.

"Ok, I'm in. What do I do to start?"

Marco bares his teeth, making him look devilish. That's always scared Val a little, but she knows it's just the way he smiles. Who Marco is- this prince-of-darkness tripping around the Haight with stacks of old books, not bothered by what others think, taking such good care of himself- Val wants that. She'll try this out and hope it works for her too.

"Let's go across the street and pick up a few things for you. I think beans, rice, yoghurt, muesli, some vegetables and fruit." He starts to clear the tea things. "Can you even cook over there at Pat's? Do you have any pots and pans? Stuff to cook with?"

Val imagines the filthy kitchen back home, its sink filled with scummy caked dishes and the odd cockroach, the greasy table and blackened floor. It's funny, since most speed freaks she knows like to scrub at things when they're high. No-one ever does that at Pat's. "Yeah... I'll find some pots and pans." She thinks of her mother's kitchen and its rows of gleaming copper pots hanging above the stove. She won't go that far, but she'll dig up what she needs. It's just keeping things clean that might be the main problem. She sighs. This is going to be harder than she thought.

Marco has slipped into his long black frock coat with the soft velvet lapels- there's even a small black rose in the buttonhole- and is waiting for her at the door. He certainly matches the décor, Val thinks. She grabs her burlap bag and follows him down the stairs to the market across the street.

2

As they walk around the small store, Marco points out various things she might want to try. There are only a few aisles, so their little spree doesn't take very long. Marco gathers the rice, beans, lentils, a brown bottle of something he says will make things taste better, a loaf of brown bread covered in tiny seeds, peanut butter, tomatoes, carrots and apples. They choose a vanilla yoghurt together and a small bag of cereal that Val thought was rabbit food. She doesn't mind the store too much. She thought it would smell like hippies- filled with the scent of incense and unwashed bodies. But no, the store smells... green and alive. She breathes in the aroma of fresh apples and carrots piled high in their bins along the front window, and feels healthier already, or maybe just warm.

Marco pays for her starter groceries, and they walk back to his apartment where Val guesses he will show her how to cook something- rice or beans or whatever. She's not hungry, but she's interested in what's next. At the apartment, Marco puts her food in his fridge- even the beans and rice, the things that don't need to go there. "Just so you don't forget anything when you head back to Pat's."

Val's always wondered- a lot of people live at that apartment, but everyone calls it Pat's place. Maybe Pat's name is on the lease. That would make sense. Sure, the rest of them pay rent and utilities, or steal toilet paper for the bathroom every now and then. But it's always been Pat's place. Even if she moved out, Val thinks it would probably still be called Pat's place.

Val stands awkwardly in the doorway between the kitchen and the parlor, uncertain what Marco has planned next. "Are you going to show me how to make something?" He grins, spooky again. "I have a better idea. Let's smoke some hash. I think you might like it."

"Is it... like H? I don't like that, so much." She plants herself in the doorway, still hoping for a cooking class. Marco laughs and erases her words with his hands. "Nonono... it's more like a light dream. Like the best parts of H- you get the visions- but without throwing up." He smiles, "You just feel... euphoric." He moves towards the parlor, and she steps out of his way. "Trust me?"

Val decides she does. She's never heard of anything bad happening around Marco- his deals are always honest, and no-one has bad reactions to the drugs he sells. Plus, now that he's doing this health food thing and he looks so good, she feels safe going along with whatever he says. "Of course. Sure, I'll try that. As long as it's not like heroin, that sounds ok to me." Marco ushers her into the parlor and says, "Take off your shoes and wait here. I'll be right back." Val sits on her favorite couch again, unwinds the laces from around her boots, and removes them both. She sniffs. Eh, Her feet are a little mushroomy, but not as bad as they could be. At least she wore clean socks. She places the boots off to the side of the couch by her burlap bag.

Marco comes back from the kitchen, carrying the tea tray again, though this time there is a wine glass, a plain white saucer with a cork on it, a stubby lit candle, and a small wood and brass inlaid box arranged across the tray's shiny stenciled surface. He sets the tray down and kneels on his pillow once more. Val leans over to see what he does next. Marco opens the hinged lid of the small box and using the tip of a sewing needle she didn't see at first, pokes and prods a tiny bead of dark brown goop from the box onto the needle tip. He closes the box and inserts the clean end of the needle into one end of the cork. Holding the cork in one hand, he picks up the lit candle and tilts it over the saucer, dripping hot wax into its center well, then affixes the clean end of the cork there, holding it in place until the wax stiffens, keeping the cork in place.

Val looks around, "Do we need a straw to smoke this?" Marco shakes his head no. "It's not like chasing the dragon. Just watch." She leans back against the couch, a little embarrassed. How would she know...? Marco holds his lighter to the hash until it flares. After a beat, he blows out the flame and places the wineglass upside down over the saucer. The hash smokes wildly and the wineglass boule fills with curlicued waves of smoke until it turns opaque. Marco leans over the tea tray, "Now do this." He places two fingers on the base of the wineglass, slightly tilts it to one side, and leans over the exposed glass bottom. Pursing his lips, he sucks hard, pulling smoke with a hiss into his lungs. He gently places the tilted edge of the wineglass back onto the saucer so that most of the smoke is still trapped inside. As he softly releases the smoke from his lungs, he says, "Now you."

Val leans over the tea tray, unsure which side of the glass she should lean into. Marco places two fingers on the base of the glass and points with a free finger to one side. She moves over, and as he tilts the glass, he says, "Inhale now! Hard! Suck it all in!" She inhales as deeply as she can, pulling in all the remaining smoke, and sits back on the couch until he tells her what to do next.

It seems like a long time passes, and Val starts to panic as the smoke expands in her lungs. She opens her eyes wide at Marco. He says, "It's ok, you can breathe. Let it out…" She does, and tastes earth at the back of her throat. That, and definitely weed as she exhales. Great, she just smoked weed like a fucking hippie. There is something sweeter lingering on her tongue though, like brown sugar or molasses, and rich, loamy earth. That's not so bad. She leans against the backrest and slumps over onto her back. Oh... this is nice. Her fingers and toes throb and loosen up. She sighs. She feels like she is floating, watching herself from above, yet firmly inside her body at the same time.

Val looks at Marco, who is leaning back on both hands and smiling softly in her direction. "Wooooowww... I feel so... good. I haven't felt this delicieuse, in I don't know how long..." She lays her head back and closes her eyes. Vivid colors ripple past the insides of her eyelids, forming shapes and images like looking through a kaleidoscope. She relaxes and watches the show.

Val has no idea how much time has passed as she's absorbing the sights and sounds swirling around her head. She hears a rustle of cloth and knows that Marco has also stretched out on the floor. She smiles gently to herself. This is very nice, a welcome change to the intensity of speed when she goes, goes, goes on it. She feels so... happy. She could stay like this forever, she thinks. She wonders if Marco needs a roommate? She really could stay here and feel this way and paint and eat health food! The thought fills her with a deep sense of warmth and sweet happiness. "Marco...?"

He sighs and waits a beat to reply. "Val...?"

"This is amazing... I'm seeing all these colors sliding around behind my eyes..." She takes a deep, easy breath, "And I feel so good."

"There is no grace. There is no guilt. Do what thou wilt is the whole of the law." He chortles gently from where is lying, stretched out on the floor.

Val tries to sit up, but decides she feels too perfect right where she is, so she just answers him, "What? What do you mean?" Marco takes a deep breath. They seem to be doing a lot of that. "That's a quote from Aleister Crowley. The Beast. The occultist whose teachings I have been studying for some time. It means that we each must follow our own path. And in the end, not judge, or be judged, by any other." He rustles as he turns over onto his side. "Which means you can do what you like for your Self. For me, I like smoking hash. For my inner Self. For you, that can mean doing speed, or not doing speed. Smoking hash or painting or eating well, or all of it. And not caring what others think or feel or say or do about any of it." He turns over onto his back again.

Val's mind spins his words into colors and shapes knocking against one another in her mind. What he said makes sense, as long as she can see his words as images, flowing and weaving freely through her thoughts. She wants to ask more, and instead she drifts off, not quite sleeping and not quite awake.

Some time passes. When Val opens her eyes, she notices that Marco has cleared the tea tray and covered her with a light dusky purple herringbone blanket. She pushes herself up to lean back against the arm of the couch and looks around. It's still light outside, so she hasn't been out for hours. This was definitely not like heroin. She didn't nod out or feel sick to her stomach, or feel completely overwhelmed. But she lost sense of time, as light and happy as she felt while drifting away... "Marco?" He's doing something in the kitchen and walks dreamily back into the parlor. "Val?" He smiles. It doesn't seem as evil as it usually does.

"What time is it?"

Marco looks at his watch, "Do you need to be somewhere?"

"No, I'm just wondering. How long were we... out?"

He laughs. "Not long. Not even an hour. See what I mean? It's not hard like H at all. And you feel so good afterwards too. No aches or shakes or any of that shit." Val stretches her arms over her head and sees what he means. She doesn't feel sick or achy in any part of her body. In fact, she still feels... peaceful. And relaxed. And happy. So weird. She wonders if she could ever give up speed and just smoke hash. That's too big to think about right now. She can deal with it later if it belongs in her future or in her life at all.

Marco opens both hands wide. "I was thinking. If you feel like it, I can show you how to cook basic lentils and rice using some of the Bragg's I got for you. That adds so much flavor." He holds one hand out. "You can stay there and relax however long you like. I don't have any appointments today. I'm just reading, so you're not in the way. Whenever you feel like it, if you want."

Val arches her back and relaxes again into the couch. "Ok... if you don't mind. I haven't felt this... happy? – in a long time. Maybe I'll just lie down for a little more..."

Marco returns to the pale gold chaise longue in the front bay window where he has been pouring over his new copy of Lectures on Yoga. It's not something he does, but he's thinking he might try bits and pieces as it suits him. He lets Val return to her half slumber and continues leafing through the book.

More time passes. When Val opens her eyes and sits up to look out the windows again, she sees the light has changed. It isn't dark outside, but golden. She loves this time of day. She wishes she had her paints and a canvas with her right now. Marco notices Val sitting up, marks the place in his book, and lays it face-down on the round marble-topped table centered between the bay windows. "Good morning sunshine." He smiles, and Val smiles in return. His smile doesn't seem threatening or evil any more to her. She interlaces her fingers together and stretches her arms overhead, palms up. She has a slight headache and she's very thirsty. And hungry. She can't remember the last time she felt hungry.

"Good... afternoon? What time is it?" She giggles. "I know. I should get a watch."

He glances at his watch. "It's just after four. Are you hungry? How about some tea to freshen up, then a little cooking lesson?" She nods earnestly, "Yes, I am very hungry." He stands, shoots the burgundy cuffs of his black velvet smoking jacket, and says, "Ok, dinner first. Then I have a little treat for us to share." Val sits up straighter, then realizes he is waiting for her, and stands. She's a little wobbly on her feet. Not high. She just hasn't rested this well in a long, long time. She lifts one foot, rotates it at the ankle, and does the same for the other. That's better. Marco gestures for her to follow him into the kitchen and he leads, tightening the sash at his waist.

For the next hour, Marco shows Val how to measure and cook a pot of rice and another pot of lentils. He apologizes for not having put beans on to soak earlier, as those take so much longer to prepare before cooking. He makes sure she understands that about beans. He cuts up a carrot and adds that to the lentils, along with a hearty splash of Bragg's. Val studies the label. Something called 'liquid aminos', whatever that is. It smells very strongly of salt and something else... manure? She wrinkles her nose. But when she sniffs at the pot of lentils cooking over a low flame, it smells good, more mushroomy and faintly herbal.

While they wait for the rice and lentils to cook, Marco makes another pot of tea, something Japanese. He serves the tea in a different set of teacups. These are pale blue, hers with a delicate design of flowers and swirls, his with flowers and bamboo sticks, and they have no handles. Marco shows her how to hold the teacup from the bottom with one hand as well as cupping the side with the other. It feels a little awkward. Val asks why use both hands when one will do? He answers this is the way you drink from these cups, so she does what he says. The tea tastes of twigs and leaves, like walking through the park on a Spring day.

Marco turned the flame off from beneath the rice a little while ago. Now he lifts the lid and pokes a fork into the rice. "Ok, this is done. See how it fluffed up when we left it alone? You turn the heat off, leave the lid on, and it keeps cooking. Make sure you do that, or you'll burn the bottom of the pot, and that's a bitch to get clean." He shows Val the forkful of rice. She doesn't really see the difference between this and what the rice looked like before, but she can follow instructions, so she'll give it a try. Mon Dieu, cooking isn't easy...

"What else do we need to do?" Val asks. She's ready to try the fragrant rice and steaming lentils now. Marco produces a beautiful black lacquered tray covered in tiny gold and red flowers and unfolds two short sets of legs tucked beneath it. Placing it on the kitchen table, he centers two light grey ceramic bowls at either end. The bowls are flecked with small white dashes, making Val long for her paints again.

Marco selects a beautiful wooden bowl from a shelf next to the sink. The wood grain almost glows. Val wonders if that's a side-effect of the hash or if the bowl is really that luminous. Marco tears leaves from a head of lettuce into bits and pieces into the bowl, chucks in a handful of sliced apple, and splashes a dollop each of vinegar and oil from two matching cruets. Wow, Val thinks, he really knows what he's doing. She's not sure she can remember it all.

Last, Marco carries the grey ceramic bowls over to the stove where he spoons servings of rice and lentils into each. He returns the bowls to the tray and snaps his fingers, "Almost forgot!" He grabs two sets of chopsticks and two cloth napkins from a ceramic cup nestled against the oil and vinegar. "Do you know how to use chopsticks?" He holds them out for her to inspect. Val shakes her head. "I'm not the best at it." Marco removes one set of chopsticks and reaches behind him to pull a fork from a drawer. He stands back, reviewing everything on the tray, decides it's all there, and says, "Shall we...?" gesturing towards the parlor.

Val assumed they would eat in the kitchen, so she says, "Oh!" and steps aside, waiting to see where he will lead her next. Her stomach has been growling for a while. Marco carries the tray into the parlor and sets it down in the middle of the room atop the gorgeous Oriental-looking rug. Val doesn't know a thing about rugs or furniture or any of Marco's treasures, but she thinks she knows quality when she sees it, and she appreciates colors and textures. His home is like a painting filled with nuance and tone. The rug is a deep Autumn-like orange with pale yellow, grey, and black filigree designs. She could dive into this rug and live in these colors, but for now, she'll sit and eat. Amazing. She's not high anymore, but all the colors and her thoughts still feel so vivid.

They dine, Val picking at the unfamiliar meal until she decides it's delicious- better than the chicken McNuggets or ice cream she usually eats without tasting, whenever she does eat. "Mmmmm... this is so good. I had no idea there is such a thing as black rice. What did you add to it?"

"Nothing. The rice is sweet. Almost nutty, can you taste that?" He holds up a mouthful of lentils and rice over his bowl. "What do you think of the lentils?" Val forks a taste into her mouth. She thinks they're a little too salty, but she likes that mushroomy flavor, and the crunch of carrots hidden in each creamy bite. "I don't think it's as easy as you said it would be. You kept adding a bit of this, a bit of that. But if you write it down for me, I can do it." She starts to take another bite but says, "I really want to."

Marco finishes his rice and lentils, and using his chopsticks, shovels salad into his bowl. Val, unused to eating regularly, feels full. She looks at Marco pleadingly, "I can't eat any more. It's delicious, but... I would like to try this salad." He nods, chewing. "Of course. Whatever you can eat, that's great. Here, give me that." He takes her bowl, jumps up, and dumps what's left in it back into the pot of lentils in the other room. He rinses out her bowl and returns to the parlor, where he sits across from her again and offers her the clean receptacle. "Take as much or as little as you like. The apples are good."

Val scoops a little lettuce and a few pieces of apple into her bowl. She's very full but wants to try everything Marco has created for her. This dinner means a lot. She's always admired him. Not sexually- Val is certain Marco is gay- but for the striking way he moves in the world and the gifts he seems to promise to share. Like this meal, the hash, and the time he's spending with her without rushing off to go someplace and be someone... She feels special around him without also feeling like she has to reciprocate. Val isn't used to that, not in the punk community where she hangs. There, if someone gives you something, they expect something in return. If someone does something for you, you owe them. There is always a price to pay, even among friends.

Val doesn't think Marco wants anything from her though. She doesn't use H, so it's not for a sale. She's not a guy, so it's not for sex. She certainly doesn't have any nice things like he owns, so it's not for trade. She happily chews the bright bite of lettuce and apple and smiles down at her bowl.

3

Marco rests his chopsticks across his bowl and leaning back, discreetly watches Val pick at a few bites of salad. He knows she's a speedster and isn't accustomed to eating regular meals, so even tiny amounts are a giant step forward. He hopes she continues to take better care of herself. Val has never struck him as hateful or racist even though she runs with that Clits gang. She paints, if he remembers correctly, which divines well for her soul once she gets past all the other stuff. If she gets past all the other stuff.

There's a lot of bad juju going on in the City these days. People are dying. People are getting jumped, scammed and knocked down in unsettling and disturbing ways. Marco has always tried to steer clear of unsavory situations, and he's been lucky that no-one has ever ripped him off. A lot of punks in the scene don't have that luck, so some are leaving the City to escape this new brutality.

He asks Val, "I heard that Babs got rolled. I guess she's dealing big time now and she got mugged?" Val picks at the last piece of apple in her bowl and decides she's had enough. "Yeah. She's got some kind of deal going with this hippie guy. She's the only distributor- that's what she calls it– for this amazing speed." She tries to lay her fork across her bowl like Marco's chopsticks, but it falls in. They both laugh. "I know you don't… do that stuff. But it's so pretty, Marco. It's this pale green, super sparkly rock. And it's. So. Good." Her heart flutters a little as she tells him about that speed. Of course she wants some. She always wants some.

"Hmm, he must be the supplier, if she's the only dealer. That's impressive. I wonder how she wrangled that? I always thought she was a, you know… minor seller. Just to support her own use. Or did I get that wrong?"

Val leans back on both hands. She wants to stretch her legs. She wants to lay down on her favorite couch again. "No, you're right. I've never thought she was a big time anything before. I just see her at shows, or sometimes she shows up at Pat's. Suddenly, she's a big dealer." She shrugs. "I don't know how that happened."

Marco stands and picks up the tray. "You all done?" Val nods and moves back to the couch. He carries the tray into the kitchen and says, "Remember, I have a surprise." She settles onto the couch and looks around the room. If she lived here, she would set up her easel over there, and keep her paints over here, and she would keep her kit and stash in that cabinet right there… Merde, stop thinking about speed for a minute! She chides herself.

Val closes her eyes and tries to regain that sense of peace and happiness she felt before. She rolls her shoulders and takes a deep breath. "Are we smoking more hash?" She calls out. Marco stops clanking dishes and things. "We could... though I have another nice surprise, something to complete our meal." She laughs and says, "I'm not trying to get more or anything. I just..." she walks over and leans against the kitchen doorway. "I just never felt anything like that before." She pauses and looks down at her bare feet. "Hey Marco, thank you so much for showing me this health food stuff. And for sharing the hash with me. I'm not trying to get more..."

He turns off the water, spins around, and pushes one of his smoking jacket sleeves over an elbow. "Val, I know. We don't know each other that well, but I can read people, and I see how you are. I don't think you're trying to pull anything over on me." He turns back to the sink and dunks one of the bowls beneath the suds. "I can finish this later. Let's have our treat." He dries his hands on a towel hanging below the sink and marshals Val back into the parlor. "Sit. We can smoke a little hash, but with some tobacco. That will go perfectly with our treat."

Val sits on what she thinks of as her couch and waits while Marco goes about the room from cabinet to armoire gathering a pair of small cut crystal glasses with short stems, a slim bottle of something dark and expensive looking, a pouch of tobacco, and the small wood and brass inlaid box. Marco lays these things out on the coffee table and sits on his velvet pillow across from Val. She considers moving to the floor and leaning back against the couch, but decides no, she's exactly where she should be.

She studies the things Marco has placed around the table. The crystal glasses refract light across the room. Val leans over to inspect them better, and sees her reflection broken into fractals and colorful shapes. She picks up the bottle and turns it around to read the label. "Vintage Port... this is our treat?" He grins as he pinches a twist of tobacco from the pouch and crumbles it into the rolling paper he holds in his free hand. "That, my dear, is a very special bottle of port. Look at the date."

Val reads further, "Quinta do Noval 1962. Is that the year?"

"That's the year I was born. The wine shop I've been foraging has a selection of ports from every year back to the late 1800's. I thought it would be a special treat to drink a good port from my birth year and see how mature we've both become." He opens the small wood and brass box and rakes the tip of a fresh pin across the oozy brick of dark hash, scraping up a small glop along the length of the pin. He lays the pin on the rolling paper against the crumbled tobacco and rolls it back and forth, transfering the hash sludge from pin to paper, where it soaks in rather quickly.

Val furrows her brow. "Wait... is it... your birthday?" Marco shakes his head as he concentrates on twisting the paper neatly around the gumbo of tobacco and hash. "No, that was two months ago. But it's the year, see? I've been saving the bottle for a special occasion. And this seems special enough." He glances up and licks the edge of the cigarette. "It's not every day someone I know takes steps to destroy the illusion around them." Val has no idea what he means by this, but she nods ok and asks, "By taking better care of myself?" Marco says, "Exactly. By disobeying the rule of the street, you are working your way towards joy. What better reason to celebrate?" He hands her the cigarette. "Here, hold this."

As Marco peels a tiny tab from the waxed cap of the bottle, Val thinks about what he just said. "Is that more of this Alison... something you were talking about earlier?" He puts the sliver of wax aside and inspects the lopsided cap. "Aleister Crowley. Yes. I can lend you a book if you like, though I don't usually. You could come here to read it? Though I have appointments, so we'd have to figure out a schedule, or you could remain in the back room if someone is here." He twists the cap, and feeling nothing give, stands and opens one of the drawers of the ornately scrolled wooden armoire. Val carefully holds the cigarette between two fingers and watches as Marco digs out a corkscrew and returns to his seat on the floor. He inserts the tip of the screw into the heavily waxed top and twists it round while holding the bottle firmly against his thigh.

"I can look for his books at the Anarchist bookstore on Haight. You think they might have something?" The thought of having to make her way here, make appointments, and hide seems like too much just to read a book she's only mildly interested in. Mostly she's curious about these quotes Marco fluidly slips into their conversation. No-one else she knows talks like this. The ideas intrigue her, but she's not sure about all the effort to learn more.

Marco eases the cork from the bottleneck. It comes away with chunks of thick broken wax. He lays that aside, folds the corkscrew, and pockets that absentmindedly. He sniffs at the open bottle. "Are you ready?" Val holds the cigarette off to one side, "Yes!"

Marco pours a lovely, dark ruby-colored draft into each glass. A whiff of blackberries and cinnamon floods the back of Val's tongue. She reaches for the glass closest to her, but Marco says, "Let's light up the hash first and try them together. I have a feeling that will be perfect."

He lifts the lighter off the tabletop and holds it in front of Val's face. She says, "Oh, oui," and places one end of the cigarette in her mouth. Marco flicks the lighter and Val inhales. She hands the cig to Marco and sucks more air in through clamped teeth. They pass it back and forth once more, then they lock eyes and Marco nods, "Let's do it..."

They lift the delicate glasses carefully, and slowly sip at the deep red, almost black liquid. Val's eyes widen. "It's like pepper! And wood... or is that the hash?" She feels doors opening behind her eyes, allowing color and flavor to flood her mind. She blinks, and the colors sway gently, swirling as before, but with flavor and less intensely. "Woah..." She wishes she could describe the experience. She hopes Marco is feeling it too.

Marco giggles. "I thought so. I mean, I know the hash is good. I was hoping the port would pair with it, like wine with food. Mmmmm... the port is excellent and just makes the hash... better. Or the hash makes the port better. Or both." He inspects the half-drawn cigarette and places it in a square marbled ashtray on the coffee table. Val looks at the ashtray and squints. Where did that come from?

Marco takes another sip of the port. "Do you taste the caramel?" Val sips again and concentrates on the sensations in her mouth. Somehow everything translates to colors swirling and melding together behind her eyes. She keeps the port in her mouth and forces it across her tongue. "I taste... nuts? And cinnamon. Is there cinnamon in this?" Marco shakes his head. "No. It's just the grapes. And something about the wood from the barrels they age the wine in. I don't know exactly how that works. I get what you're tasting too- something spicy." He sighs and takes another sip.

Val glances at the bay windows and notices the fading light outside. "Oh, the light. It's so pretty..." She raises her glass towards the purplish dusky light. Marco moves the small table between them out of the way and sits closer to the couch, leaning back on one hand with his glass of port in the other. Val leans back against the arm of the couch, her long legs at an angle so her feet dangle above the carpet below. Marco reaches up and places one hand on the arch of her foot. He lightly brushes his thumb across her metatarsals. It feels nice, but Val isn't sure what to do. Is this a come on? Isn't Marco gay?

She tries to sit up, but Marco presses his forearm against hers, softly keeping her in place, "No, if you don't mind..." He puts his nearly empty glass of port down on the table behind him. Then he turns back to Val and touches her foot again with both hands. "I really love a beautiful foot. It's just... something I admire. Is this ok, if I touch them?" She wants to put her port glass down too, but she can't reach the table easily, lying at this angle. "Um... this is a little weird. Aren't you gay?" Marco presses into the arch of her foot with both thumbs, gently pressing from heel to ball, heel to ball. It feels so good, and mon Dieu, the colors...

Marco clears his throat. "No, I'm not gay. Not exactly. But I'm not straight either. I'm what you call asexual. I just don't have any interest in sex, really." Val takes another sip of the port and places the foot of the small glass on her sternum. She closes her eyes to take this in. "So... no sex? At all? Not even, quoi, alone? Mon Dieu, that feels amazing."

Marco shifts so he can lay Val's foot atop one knee. He continues to knead and stroke her foot, heel to ball, and across the ball, side to side. "Not even alone. I've had sex before, of course. But years ago, I stopped trying to figure out which way my sexuality should go. If any way at all." He pauses as he presses deeply into her arch. "Then I realized I just wasn't interested. I mean, I have passion, and I get aroused, but I don't need to do anything about it. 'Each star must go on its own orbit.' Another Crowley saying." He smiles.

"But this... I have... it's not exactly a foot fetish. It's just- I find feet very erotic, and I feel a release of energy when I caress a beautiful foot." Val shoots a look at Marco's groin. He chuckles. "I don't have a hard on. I'm turned on by this... but it's deeper than sexuality. It's a deeper orbit, if that makes sense."

Val sighs. "I guess. I don't understand exactly. But..." she tries to find words that match what she's feeling. "I feel safe. I don't think you're coming on to me. I have all these amazing colors and tastes and sounds in my head, all because you are being... so kind and generous with your day. And now this," she kicks her foot into his hand. "This is almost better than the hash and port."

Marco digs into the ball of her foot. Val feels tiny explosions beneath his thumbs. Is that her bones? This is so strange, but so good too. What did Marco say earlier? 'Do what thou will' or something like that. She says, "Ok... do what thou will... do it til you're satisfied." Marco laughs. "That's funky." Val closes her eyes as he pulls at her toes, one at a time, gently. Two pop and he caresses the length of each toe. "That's a funk song, I think. 'Do it til you're satisfied.'" He laughs again. "Though it's something Crowley might have said too."

Val loses herself in the rubbing and stroking, allowing each sensation to flower in colors behind her eyelids. Marco switches to her other foot, giving that equal attention.

Sometime later, he pauses and says, "Wait a second. Don't move." He goes into another room for a minute, and returns, quietly sitting on the floor by her feet. "I'm going to paint your toenails, ok?" Of course, she thinks. "Ok." She takes another sip of the port and hands it to him, worried she might fall asleep and spill what's left in the glass. Marco takes the glass, and Val nestles back into the couch. How did she get here? She doesn't feel awkward at all, just... satisfied.

She smells the lacquer as he opens the bottle, reminding her of her paints. She hopes the color is nice but can't open her eyes to look. She feels a little thrill that he is decorating her, and she will carry something of him on her when she leaves. Something that no-one else will see. As he holds her foot and paints each toenail with light strokes that are cold to the touch, Marco clears his throat. "You really have beautiful feet. I'm surprised, honestly. You're always wearing heavy boots. I thought they would be rough."

Val smiles, I have beautiful feet, she thinks. He clears his throat again. "I have a proposition for you." She thinks, 'I didn't hear that right', and asks, "A proposition...?"

He finishes the toes on one foot and gently places that ankle over the armrest, turning his attention to the other foot. "Yes. A proposition. You want to be healthier. I enjoy cooking simple meals. We seem to enjoy each other's company. What if we make this a regular thing? You come over, I cook, we can smoke some hash or not. Drink a glass of wine or port, or not. I only ask that you allow me to tend to your feet." He pauses. "I mean, let me massage them, paint your nails. I have some beautiful Japanese slippers you could wear... Again. Nothing sexual. But I would truly enjoy that. It would... get me off without getting me off, if that makes sense. I don't want to make you uncomfortable. I just think we could both benefit from this arrangement."

Val observes the colors shifting this way and that behind her eyes. They are peaceful and excited at once. There is nothing jagged or anxious about the way the colors move or about the shapes they take. She trusts the colors, so she trusts Marco. Not once has he forced her to do anything she doesn't want to do. He has been so kind and has shared so much with her. She feels precious. Ok, she'll enter this arrangement and see where it goes. Why not? At least she will eat healthier and maybe get new ideas to paint. She realizes Marco is waiting for a reply. She opens one eye and watches him, as he is bent over her feet.

"So... I have to tell you. This is a little strange." She waves one hand towards her feet. "No-one has ever done anything like this to my feet before. Or to any part of me." Marco purses his lips. "That's a shame."

Val shakes her hands, "Nono, that's not what I mean! I mean... this is... obsessive? Is that the right word? To have you...more than like..." she searches for a word.

"Dote?" Marco asks.

"Yes, 'dote'." She tries to explain, "Without there being sex. I read a story somewhere about a man who had this foot fetish. But it was all sex. This doesn't feel like that at all. Like you said."

Marco runs the tip of his long pinky nail along one of her feet and waits for more. Val tries to catch his eye. "Part of me thinks this is strange because I've never seen you like this before. We've never even hung out this long. But another part of me feels very safe. And satisfied. And I'm not thinking 'When is my next shot of speed'? I don't know if that's the hash or the port or the food, or what. I just know there are all these beautiful colors behind my eyes. And none of them are exploding or agitée. They are peaceful, making me feel calm and wanting to paint what I see. If I see these peaceful colors, this must be a good, safe thing."

Marco squeezes her foot. "That sounds like a new language- all your own- when you see these colors as feelings or thoughts. 'The joy of life consists of the enjoyment of every new experience.' I like you Val. Let's enjoy this together." Marco looks around the parlor. "I was going to suggest you bring some paints, canvases, whatever, over too. But... I don't think there is a good place for that. Do you mind not being able to paint here?"

Val wiggles her toes and stretches her arms over her head. "No, that's fine. I live at Pat's. All my things are there. I will paint there too." She closes her eyes again to stay closer to the colors there. "I like the idea of coming here and taking small vacances from everything else. To read and eat healthy. To have you dote my feet."

"Dote on your feet," he corrects her. "Let's do that. You can choose whatever books you want to read. Like I said, you'll just have to stay in the other room when I have appointments." He gestures towards the back room. "I'll cook. I'll dote." He smiles. "You eat. You speak your language of color with yourself. We can just do it til we're satisfied."

He partly sings the last part. "Oh, maybe this interest you!" He jumps up and rummages in another drawer at the scrolled armoire. When he returns, he moves the small table back into its place next to her couch and clears their bacchanalian debris to one side. He lays a small rectangular sack embroidered with very simple large red stitches in a native pattern of some kind on the center of the table. Val can make out a bird, and is that corn? She rolls over onto her side. She thinks if she sits up, she'll lose the colors, which are already beginning to fade. Marco holds both hands over the small rectangular sack, framing it beneath his fingers. There is a thick red string at one end of the sack that he pulls open. He draws out a thick deck of cards and lays them on top of the emptied sack. The top card has an image of a man with his legs outstretched and a tiger or lion climbing up one leg. The man has horns and there are birds and butterflies swirling around him. The colors are rich and jewel-like. Val sits up.

"This is a tarot deck?" She looks to Marco and he nods in confirmation. "I've never seen this one before. It's beautiful." She reads the title of the card at the top of the deck, 'The Fool'. She reaches for the deck and pauses, with her hand held over the cards. She knows some people are proprietorial with their tarot decks. You can't touch their decks unless invited. Marco fans the cards out onto the table for her. "Go ahead." Val reaches into the middle of the deck and pries a card out from the rest. She studies it for a moment, taking in its rich colors and imagery, then turns the card to show Marco.

"Ah. The Knight of Swords." He smiles conspiratorially at Val. "That is perfect." She furrows one brow. "Can you tell me what this means?" He says, "Of course. Hang on." He jumps up again– Val notices how spry he is after looking so much like an old man when she saw him only months before. He slides a large paperback book from a stack on the table against the bay windows and returns to his spot on the rug. The book falls open at a page that reads Knight of Swords, with a black and white copy of the image she holds in her hand. Marco peruses the words written on the page and reads out, "This is a symbol of passionate thinking. These three swallows," he points to the three small birds at the bottom of the card, "represent the union of mind, heart and action. They serve as reminders that focus, will, and attention must be aligned before a goal can be obtained."

He looks at Val and grins. "Do you get it? Your desire to eat well must be aligning with your innate artistic senses. You come here and eat, smoke, drink, relax, and fire up all these colorful feelings and thoughts... You succumb to what the universe intends for you, as you align yourself with those intentions." Val shrugs her shoulders. She doesn't understand any of this magic mumbo jumbo. The one thing that does make sense to her is the thing he said about firing up her colorful thoughts and feelings. Something about how if she makes her mind up to come here and eat healthy, the universe– or whatever– will bring these colors back to her.

"So… if I want to eat healthy, I get rewarded with all these glorious colors in my head?"

Marco puts the book down. "Sort of. The card is saying that you are master of your own intentions and passions. And that if you put your mind to whatever it is that you truly want, you will receive the gifts you so desire." Val enjoys Marco's lyrical speech when he talks about things he obviously knows well and is passionate about. She thinks she understands what he is saying. She points to the wings spread out in four directions on the knight's back. "This looks to me like North, South, East, West. Like this Knight has a choice which direction to go? I can choose my direction and that will take me where I am supposed to be?"

Marco raises one eyebrow and pushing his lower lip out, nods. "Yes… that's a good way of seeing it." He taps two fingers on the table. "I would say pick another card. But I think this is enough for now. I think this," he closes the book, "would be a great place for you to start with your reading. There are so many images and colors. The artist was Lady Frieda Harris. She painted each and every one of the cards for this deck. It's called the Deck of Thoth, and it's my favorite. I have other tarot decks, but this is the deck I use for daily meditations. And the card you chose was perfect."

Val wants to look at all the cards, to take in all the deep colors and images. She sits back. This will be like a gift waiting for her the next time she comes. "I love this. Yes, I would like very much to read this book and... may I use your deck? Or...?" Marco looks up, thinking. "Let's get you your own deck. That hippie bookstore up on Haight you mentioned earlier- they have decks there and should have this one." He reaches for the Knight of Swords and Val places it in his hand. He lays it atop The Fool, cuts the deck in two, and settles the two halves together. As he slides the cards back into the rough-hewn pouch and closes the red string, he says, "What are you doing tomorrow? We could meet up there, and if they don't have the deck, there's that occult store. They will definitely have it. Just to make sure you get the right deck. Who knows? Some other deck may jump out at you."

Val thinks. "I have to pick up my pay from the City. Other than that, no plans. Our skate isn't until Saturday." She peers over the edge of the couch for her socks and boots. "Marco... I need to head back to Pat's. I need to paint. I'm not being rude?" Marco stands and picks up the cork from the end of the table. He pries a large chunk of wax off the end and forces the cork back into the top of the bottle.

"Do what thou wilt, Val, my dear. That is the whole of the law." He opens one of the doors of the ornate armoire and places the port bottle next to other bottles of assorted shapes and sizes. He gathers the two glasses and wax debris and carries them into the kitchen. Val thinks she understands what he means when he says that now.

He calls out from the kitchen, "I have an appointment at twelve that should be done by one. Can you meet at two, to be on the safe side? Let's just meet at the occult store. I know they'll have a selection and the Thoth deck will definitely be one of them."

Val admires her toes. He has painted them a lustrous, sparkling red. She reluctantly pulls on her socks and boots. "That's perfect." She wraps the long laces around her ankles, ties them off, and stands. "My food...?" She takes a step towards the kitchen as Marco appears in the doorway holding the bag of groceries. "Here you go." He hands her the bag and walks her to the apartment door. He looks around his parlor and as he opens the door, he pauses, "You know... I've been thinking about hanging some art in here. Maybe... let's see what you paint after you start reading Aleister Crowley. I might commission something."

Val has to catch her breath. She has never considered selling her art before. She paints because she is driven to pick up a brush. Maybe she'll walk all the way back to Pat's to give herself more time to dream about all the new possibilities that have unfolded today. She feels like she's stepped into a different world. Maybe it's the hash, or the port, or the food. Or maybe she shouldn't try to figure it out, and just do it til she's satisfied.

About the author

Photo by Paula Batzella

Ruby grew up in the foothills of Northern CA and the West Texas flatlands, riding horses in the back woods near Folsom Prison, and singing with family on the back porch. She attended SDSU at fifteen- studying electrical engineering and drama- then stumbled into life on the streets of San Francisco, enchanted by all the grime and glitz, the drugs and wild nights, even the discordance and insanity of life as a punk in those early days.

Moving on, Ruby co-founded the North Coast California Earth First! in Arcata, CA while attending Humboldt State, and fished across Alaskan waters. Eventually, she moved to Seattle, WA where she opened a series of restaurants, then transitioned from restaurateur to singer/songwriter when she started the roots-rockabilly band Ruby Dee and the Snakehandlers in 2002. Thrice Grammy-considered, they tour the world and produce award-winning records.

In 2023, Ruby wrote Bag of Tricks after reconnecting with old punk friends and reminiscing about those lost years. Most of what she wrote came from events that really occurred, though Ruby took liberties and changed some details because she could.

BAG OF TRICKS

Mixed Stories of Life as a San Francisco

Punk in the early 80's

BOOK ONE OF A PUNK TRILOGY

Ruby Dee Philippa

MY PUNK ROCK LIFE

The Photography of Marla Watson

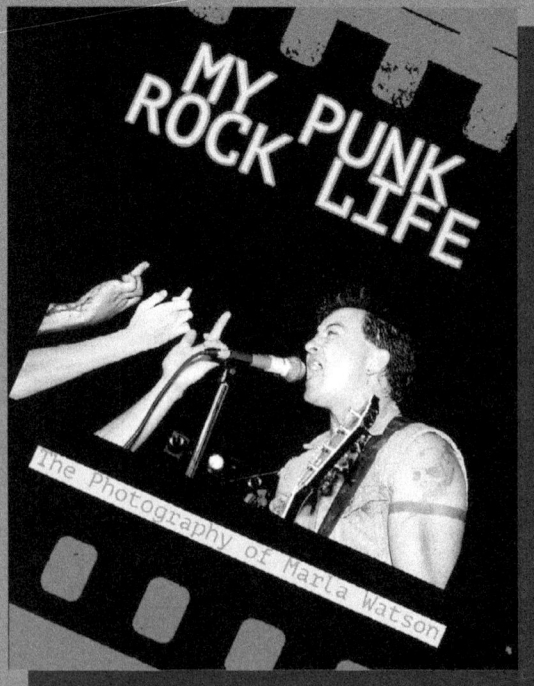

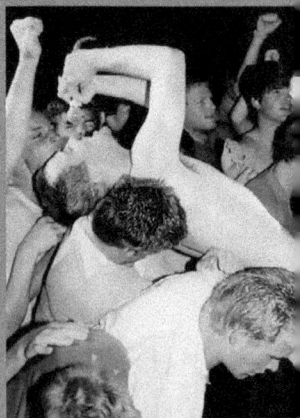

MY PUNK ROCK LIFE:
THE PHOTOGRAPHY
OF MARLA WATSON

MYPUNKROCKLIFE.COM
EARTHISLANDBOOKS.COM

Ei EARTH
ISLAND
BOOKS

PUNK
ROCK LIFE
PRESS